SPEAK
ANTIQUE

DATE DUE			

SPEAK
ANTIQUE

A Pronunciation Guide
and Glossary
for Arts & Antiques

DONNA M. STONE

WILLIAM L. BAUHAN, PUBLISHERS
DUBLIN, NEW HAMPSHIRE

2001

Stone, Donna M., 1938–
    Speak Antique: a pronunciation guide and glossary to arts and antiques / Donna M. Stone
        p. cm.
    ISBN 0-87233-127-X
    1. Art--Terminology--Pronunciation. 2. Antique--Terminology--Pronunciation. 1.
Title.

N34 .S76 2000
701'.4--dc21

99-462156

William L. Bauhan, Publishers
P.O. Box 443
Dublin, NH 03444
Toll Free: 877-832-3738
www.bauhanpublishing.com

Printed and Bound in the United States of America

To Elizabeth, Jon and Jennifer
My Children

*I wish to express my deep and loving gratitude to Niki Craig
for her collaboration on this book. Without her diligence and loyalty,
this manuscript would never have been completed.*

Preface

This is a book designed to take the guesswork out of pronouncing difficult words related to the arts. As a gallery owner and former antique appraiser/lecturer, I felt uncomfortable using words not familiar to my audiences.

Such are the hurdles we all encounter in this business which uses terms with foreign origins, not to mention words from different historical periods, regions, and countries.

I became aware of a need for such a handbook after I had consulted numerous art and antiques dictionaries, none of which included phonetic pronunciation.

This book gives the phonetic pronunciation and a brief description of the subject. For more detailed information, the reader should consult one of the many fine art and antiques dictionaries.

It is my hope that this book will appeal both to the professional and novice, giving them confidence to express themselves clearly in the sophisticated field of art and antiques.

Consultants

The following persons supplied information on the pronunciation of names in the languages listed in parentheses after their names (the authors, however, being alone responsible for the interpretation of the information supplied and for the pronunciations as they appear in this book):

Niki Whitley Craig of St. Francis High School, Louisville, Kentucky
    and Riverview Elementary School, Murfreesboro, N.C.
    (French, Spanish, Italian, Greek)
Margot de Nijs Cruz of Castricum, The Netherlands
    (Dutch, German, Flemish)
The Reverend John K. Dixon (Korean)
Martha Kirwan Ford of Dublin, Ireland (Irish)
Barbara Glick of Ahoskie, N.C. (German)
Michael Goldentul of Moscow, U.S.S.R. (Russian)
Ahmet Gultekin of Louisville, Kentucky (Turkish)
Kevin Herbert of Aberdare, South Wales (Welsh)
Iraj Khodadadegan of Iraj, Ltd. Oriental Rugs,
    Louisville, Kentucky (Persian)
Gitte Lykke Madsen of Sønderborg, Denmark
    (Danish, Swedish, Norwegian)
Matthew Slatkin of Louisville, Kentucky (Chinese)
Makiko Tashrio of the Christian Women's University, Tokyo, Japan
    and the University of Louisville, Kentucky (Japanese)
Helga Vinson of West Berlin, West Germany (German)
Katerina Katsarka Whitley of Thessaloniki, Greece
    and New York, NY (Greek)
Sun Xi of the Guangzhou Foreign Language Institute, China
    and the University of Louisville, Kentucky (Chinese)

Acknowledgments

I wish to express my grateful appreciation to these consultants:

Dr. Robert St. Clair, Department of English & Linguistics, University of Louisville, Kentucky

William Morgan, Professor of Architecture, Roger Williams University, Bristol, Rhode Island

Carole Rich, Associate Professor of Journalism, University of Alaska, Anchorage, Alaska

Jacque Parsley, Artist, Director of Bank One Gallery, Louisville, Kentucky

Gail Gilbert, Art Librarian, Margaret M. Bridwell Art Library, University of Louisville, Kentucky

Kathy Moore, Assistant to the Art Librarian, Margaret M. Bridwell Art Library, University of Louisville, Kentucky

Marjorie Greenberg, Research Associate for Ceramics; Old Barracks Museum, Trenton, New Jersey

Guide to Pronunciation

1. There are several ways to pronounce a word. The most common pronunciations were chosen.

2. If there is a discrepancy between the original pronunciation and the anglicized pronunciation of a foreign term, both have been included (the anglicized version preceding the original).

3. When an English word can serve as a phonetic example, it is put in quotation marks.

4. The stressed syllable is capitalized.

5. In correct French pronunciation all syllables are stressed equally, the last one being lengthened. Since we are anglicizing the pronounciation of these terms, we have indicated that the last syllable is stressed.

6. Superscript letters mean that the syllable receives little or no stress.
    Example: table (French)   TAH bl^{uh}

7. A letter in parentheses signifies that the letter is barely pronounced.
    Example: Deux   du(r)

8. The Wade-Giles pronunciation is used for the Chinese terms.

9. Proper names have been omitted except in cases where their names are synonymous with their work.

10. The pronunciation symbols in our key are the pronunciation symbols used by most dictionaries.

11. The plural of the term is added if the word has an irregular plural ending.

12. Languages are abbreviated as followed:

Afg.	Afghanistan
Amer.	American
Anat.	Anatolian
Aus.	Austrian
Chi.	Chinese
Dan.	Danish
Dut.	Dutch
Eng.	English
Flem.	Flemish
Fr.	French
Ger.	German
Gk.	Greek
Heb.	Hebrew
Ir.	Irish
It.	Italian
Jap.	Japanese
Kor.	Korean
Lat.	Latin
Nor.	Norwegian
Pak.	Pakistan
Per.	Persian
Rus.	Russian
Sp.	Spanish
Swe.	Swedish
Tur.	Turkish
Turk.	Turkoman

Key to Pronunciation

Our Symbol	Example
ah	father
ay *or* aye	bay
a	bat
aw	saw
ai	air
e *or* eh	bed
eye, ie,	eye
i..e	tide
ee	feet
ew	dew
i, ih	tip
o, oh, *or* oe	toe
oo	too
ow	now

Our Symbol	Example
oy	boy
ue	*rue* (French)
uh	bug
ur	word
ure	pure
ch	church
g *or* gh	go
<u>h</u>	Bach (guttural h)
j	Joe
(m) *or* (n)	nasalized "m" or "n"
sh	shoe
th	think
<u>th</u>	this
y	yes
zh	garage

SPEAK
ANTIQUE

A

Abaciscus	**AB** uh **SIS** "cuss"	In architecture, a small abacus.
Abadeh	**AB** ah day	A Persian rug woven in the village of Abadeh.
Abat-jour	a ba-**ZHOOR**	(Fr.) A candle-shade.
Abattant	a ba **TAH(N)**	(Fr.) A term for a drop-front or fall-front panel.
Abat-voix	a ba-**VWAH**	(Fr.) A type of canopy used over pulpits.
Abbatial	uh **BAY** shul	The buildings which constitute an abbey.
Abbazzo	ah **BAHT** soh	(It.) A rough draft or sketch.
Abolla	uh "**BOWL**" uh	A woolen cloak worn by the ancient Romans.
Abraum	**AB** rawm	A red ocher.
Abraxas	uh **BRAK** sus	A mystic word found on amulets of the late Greco-Roman world.
Abricotier Wood	ab ree ko tee **AY**	A hard, compact, yellowish-colored wood of the apricot tree.
Abtsbessingen	ahpts **BESS** ing en	An early German faïence factory founded at Abtsbessingen, Thuringia during the first half of the 18th century.
Abura Wood	ah "**BURR**" ah	A light brown-colored West African wood.

Acacia Faux Wood	uh **KAY** shuh **FOE**	*A hard, yellow and greenish-striped wood from the common locust tree.*
Acajou	**AK** uh zhew	*(Fr.) A term for mahogany.*
Acanthus	uh **CAN** thus *pl.* -thigh	*An ornamentation representing or suggesting the leaves of the Mediterranean species acanthus spinosus.*
Accouchement Set	a coosh **MAH(N)**	*A nine, or more usually five piece ceramic service, arranged to fit together forming a vase or urn.*
Accoudoir	a coo **DWAHR**	*(Fr.) The ledge of a window.*
Acetabulum	"ass" i **TAB** yuh lum *pl.* -luh	*A small ancient Roman vessel to hold vinegar.*
Acheiropoeitos	ah <u>hee</u> roh **PEE** ee tohs	*A sacred image or object believed to have been created without human intervention.*
Acroterium	ak ruh **TEER** ee um *pl.* -uh	*A roof decoration on the peaks and corners of Greek temples. Also applied to furniture.*
Acus	"**A**" "cuss"	*A pin used to fasten garments and also used to pass through plaited hair.*
À deux crayons	ah du(r) cray **YOH(N)**	*(Fr.) Drawing in crayons using two colors (red and black).*
Adytum	"**ADD**" i tum *pl.* -tuh	*In ancient Greece, a sacred part of a temple reserved only for the priests.*
Aedicula *or* Aedicule	eh "**DICK**" yuh luh *pl.* -lee **ED** uh cule	*A niche for a statue.*

Aegean Art	ee **JEE** un	*Art work developed by early cultures living around the Aegean Sea, i.e. Mycenaean, Minoan, and Cycladic.*
Aesculapius	**ES** kyuh **LAY** pee us	*In Greek mythology, the god of medicine and healing.*
Affenkapelle	ahf^en kah peh luh	*(Ger.) A series of monkey porcelain figures first modelled at Meissen.*
Afghan Bokhara	**AF** gan bo **KAHR** uh boo **KAHR** uh	*An oriental rug of Turkoman origin.*
Afshar	**AF** shahr	*An oriental rug of Persian origin.*
Agalloch Wood	uh **GAL** uck **AG** uh lock	*A soft wood of varied coloration from an East Indian tree.*
Agalmatolite	a gull **MAD'L** ite	*A soft stone used by Chinese for carvings.*
Agate Ware	**AG** it	*Pottery made with a mixture of clays to resemble agate.*
Agra	**AH** gruh **AH** greh	*An oriental rug from the Uttar Pradesh state in Northern India.*
Agraffe	uh **"GRAPH"**	*An ornamented clasp for armor or clothing.*
Aigrette	**"A"** gret	*An ornament of plumes or gems worn on a hat or in the hair.*
Aikuchi	**EYE** kuh chee	*A Japanese knife or dagger made without a guard.*
Ailanto Wood	eye **LAHN** toe	*A hard, reddish wood also called 'tree of heaven', native to East India and China.*

Ailettes	ay **LET**	*In armor, protective plates attached to the shoulders.*
Ajouré	ah zhew **RAY**	*Pertaining to metalwork that has been elaborately pierced or perforated.*
Akaji Kinga	ah kah jee keen gah	*A Japanese term for a type of porcelain decoration carried out in gold or silver on a red ground.*
Ajarcara	ah h̲ahr **KAH** rah	*(Sp.) Ornamental brickwork in relief.*
Akhisar or Ak-Hissar	**AHK**-issar	*An Anatolian rug woven in this village near Bergama.*
Albarello	ahl bah **RELL** oh *pl.* -ee	*A cylindrical, majolica jar used for storing dry drugs.*
Alcazar	**AL** kah zahr ahl **KAH** thahr	*A Spanish or Moorish fortress or palace.*
Alcora	ahl **KOH** rah	*A faïence factory founded at Alcora, Valencia, Spain in 1727.*
Alençon Point	"**ALAN**" sahn uh **LEN** sahn	*A fine French needlepoint lace.*
Alercé Wood	ah lair **SAY**	*A soft, reddish-brown wood of the Sandarac tree from central Chile.*
Alicatados	ah lee kah **TAH** dose	*In ceramics, a Spanish term for cutwork.*
Alisier Wood	uh **LEE** zee ay	*A hard, white-colored wood of the white beam tree.*
Alla Porcellana	**AH** lah por chel **LAH** nah	*(It.) A blue foliate scroll motif used on the backs of plates and dishes from some majolica factories.*

Allecret	al **KREH**	A half suit of light plate armor.
Almique Wood	ahl **MEE** kay	A hard, reddish-brown wood of a West African tree.
Almoner's Cupboard	**AL** muh ner	A livery cupboard, formerly used as a storage place for food.
Alpujarra	al poo **HAHR** uh	A Spanish hand-loomed peasant rug or bedspread.
Alsace	al **SAYSE** al **ZAHS**	A provincial style of furniture named for a region in France.
Altai Rug	**AL** tay **AL** tie	An oriental rug from central Asia.
Altare	ahl **TAH** ray	Altare glass industry founded in Genoa, Italy during the Middle Ages.
Alto-Rilievo	alto-ree **LEAVE** oh ahl toh-ree lee **EH** voh	(It. 'high relief') Deeply carved relief sculpture in stone, wood, etc.
Altrohlau	ahl troh low	A ceramic center in Altrohlau, near Carlsbad, Austria.
Altwasser	ahlt vah "sir"	(Ger.) A porcelain factory founded at Altwasser, Silesia in 1845.
Amandier Wood	a mah(n) d^(ee)**AY**	A hard, yellowish wood of the almond tree.
Amaranth Wood	**AM** uh ranth	A hard, purplish-red wood from Guiana.
Amassette	a mah **SET**	(Fr.) An instrument of wood or horn with which painters mixed their colors on the palette.
Amberina	am buh **REEN** uh	Art glass, having transparent colors from pale amber to ruby.

Amboina Wood or Amboyna	am **BOY** nuh	A hard wood with curly or mottled grain from Southern Asia.
Ambry	**AM** bree	An enclosed niche or cupboard.
Ambulante	ah(m) bue lah(n)t	(Fr.) A small portable stand or table generally used for serving tea, etc.
Ame-Gussuri	ah mee-gou sou ree	A Japanese term for a dark brown glaze, used on pottery made at the Seto kilns in the early 14th century.
Amethystine	am uh **THYS** tin -teen/tine	A purple or violet quartz or glass used as a gem.
Amice	**AM** iss	An ecclesiastical vestment worn around neck and shoulders.
Amorino	ah muh **REE** no pl. -nee	(It. 'little cupid') An ornament used in European decorative art, depicting an infant cupid.
Amortissement	a "more" tees **MAH(N)**	(Fr.) In architecture, a type of ornament used to terminate a building.
Amphora	**AM** fuh ruh pl. -ree	An ancient Greek storage jar.
Ampulla	am **PULL** uh pl. -ee	A small vessel for oil or perfume.
Amritsar	am **RIT** sir	An oriental rug woven in India.
Amulet	**AM** "you" lit	A charm used as protection against evil or injury.
Anadem	**AN** uh dum	A Greek term for a garland or wreath worn on the head.

Anaglyph	**AN** uh glif	*Low relief sculpture. In jewelry, cameos and gems sculptured or embossed in low relief.*
Anamorphosis	an uh "**MORE**" fuh sis	*A distorted drawing that appears in natural form when seen at a particular angle.*
Ananaspokal	ah nah **NAHS** po **KAHL**	*(Ger.) A term for pineapple cup.*
Anatolian	"anna" **TOE** lee un	*An oriental rug of Turkish origin.*
Ancona	ahn "**COH**" nah	*(It.) An altarpiece.*
Andiers	ah(n) d^{ee}**AY**	*Metal stands for holding logs in a fireplace.*
Andirons	**AN** "die" "urns"	*Supports for holding logs.*
Anelace	"**ANNA**" lace	*A short sword or dagger.*
Angevin	ah(n)zh **VA(N)**	*(Fr.) A type of architecture with characteristic dropped arches.*
Angleterre	ah(n) gl^{uh} **TAIR**	*A French silk taffeta that is highly finished. Sometimes referred to as Point de Bruxelles.*
Angoulême Pottery	ah(n) goo **LEM**	*(Fr.) A faïence factory started at Angoulême, Charente, in 1748.*
Angoumois	ah(n) goo **MWAH**	*A provincial style of furniture, named for a former French province.*
An-hua	ahn-whah	*(Chi.) In ceramics, a term meaning 'secret decoration'.*
Animaliers, Les	"**ANNA**" muh lee ur ah nee mah lee **AY**, lays	*A group of French animal sculptors of the early 19th c.*

Anise Wood	"**ANN**" ess	A hard, grey wood from China.
Annealing	uh "**KNEEL**" ing	The process of heating a material (glass, metal, earthen ware, etc.) to relieve internal stress.
Ansbach	ahns bahk	(Ger.) A porcelain factory founded at Ansbach, Bavaria in 1758.
Anthemion	ann **THEE** mee un *pl.* -uh	A stylized honeysuckle flower and leaf ornament, derived from classical architecture.
Antimacassar	**AN** tee muh **CASS** er	An ornamental covering on furniture to prevent wear or soiling.
Antimony	**AN** tuh **MOE** nee	A brittle metal with a silvery lustre.
Ao-Bizen	ah oh-bee zen	In Japanese ceramics, the name given to a greyish-green clay Bizen ware.
Aogai	ah oh gah ee	A Japanese lacquer inlaid with mother-of-pearl.
Aoi Tsuba	ah oh ee tsoo bah	A Japanese form of sword guard.
Apadana	a puh "**DONNA**"	The great hall of a Persian palace.
Apophyge	uh **PAHF** i jee	In architecture, a small concave curve joining the column shaft to its base.
Appliqué	**AP** luh kay ap luh **KAY**	(Fr.) A term for a wall sconce or bracket. Also, material cut out and applied to a larger piece.
Aprey	a **PRAY**	(Fr.) A faïence factory founded in 1744 at Haute-Marne.

Apulian	uh **PYOU** lee un	Ancient Greek pottery found at Apulia, Italy.
Aquamanile	"aqua" muh **NIGH** lee	A medieval bronze ewer used for washing hands.
Aquarelle	"aqua" **RELL**	A watercolor or drawing executed in transparent colors.
Arabesque	ah ruh **BESK**	A rhythmic, linear surface decoration, composed of foliage and light scrollwork.
Araucaria Wood	a roh **KA** ree uh	A soft, light-brown wood mainly from Brazil, Paraguay, and Argentina.
Arbalest	"R" buh list	A medieval cross-bow.
Arc-Boutant	"ark"-boo **TAH(N)**	(Fr.) In architecture, a flying buttress.
Archaic	"r" **KAY** ik	The Greek art period of the 6th century B.C.
Archature	"R" kuh chur	In architecture, a small or blind arcade.
Archebanc	arsh ba(n)k	(Fr.) An early wooden bench with back and arms.
Architrave	"R" kuh trave	The lowest section of the entablature which rests immediately on the capital of a column or pilaster.
Archivolt	"R" kuh "volt"	The molded or decorated band surrounding an arch.
Arcus Ecclesiae	"R" "cuss" eek **LEE** zee "eye"	An arch which divides the nave from the choir.
Ardebil Rug	"R" deh "bill"	An oriental rug of Persian origin.

Argand Lamp	"**R**" gand	A type of oil lamp with chimney and tubular wick.
Argentan	"**R**" jun tan	German silver; an alloy of nickel, copper, and zinc. Also, a French needlepoint lace.
Argyle or Argyll	"**R**" "guy"l	An English silver gravy-warmer resembling a coffee pot.
Arita Ware	ah **REED** uh	(Jap.) Porcelain made in Arita. Also known as Imari or Imari-Yaki.
Armadio	"r" **MAH** dee oh	(It.) A tall, movable cupboard.
Armario	"r" **MAH** ree oh	(Sp.) A massive cupboard, often having two long cupboard doors.
Armet	"r" meh	In armor, a completely enclosed helmet, globular in shape.
Armoire	"r" mwahr	(Fr.) A tall, massive cupboard or wardrobe.
Armoire à Deux Corps	"r" mwahr ah du(r) kor	(Fr.) A double-bodied cupboard.
Arquebus	"r" kuh **BUEZ**	See Harquebus.
Arqueta	"r" **KAY** tah	(Sp.) A small chest, often for storing jewels.
Arras Ceramics	"**R**" iss	(Fr.) A soft paste porcelain factory founded at Arras, Pas de Calais in 1770.
Arras	"**R**" iss	(Fr.) A coarse French bobbin lace manufactured at Arras from the 16th century. Also, a tapestry weaving center at Arras from the 14th century.

Arretine Ware	**A** ruh tine **A** ruh teen	An ancient Italian red-glazed, terra-cotta pottery.
Arriccio	ah "**REACH**" ee oh	Formerly in fresco painting, the second coating of plaster applied to the wall.
Arsedine	"**R**" suh deen "**R**" suh dine	Dutch gold: gold-colored alloy of copper and zinc.
Art Engagé	"art" ah(n) ga **ZHAY**	(Fr.) A 19th century term to characterize art with political or social implications.
Art Moderne	"art" moh **DAIRN**	(Fr.) A term to describe a style derived from the Paris Exposition of 1925.
Art Nouveau	"art" noo **VOH** ahr noo **VOH**	An art style and period of the late 19th and early 20th century characterized primarily by curvilinear themes derived from natural forms.
Artesonado	"r" tay so **NAH** doe	(Sp.) A type of pine panelled ceiling of Moorish origin.
Artois	"r" **TWAH**	A style of furniture named after an old French province.
Aryballos or Aryballus	a ruh **BAL** us pl. -loy	An ancient Greek globular container for holding oils.
Aschbach	ahsh bahk	A pottery factory at Aschbach, northern Bavaria, founded in 1829.
Ashi	ah shee	Loops on a Japanese single-edged sword that allowed cording to pass through.
Ashikaga	ah shee kah gah	A Japanese time period (1333-1573).

Assisi Work	ah **SEE** see ah **SEE** zee	An embroidery having unworked motifs outlined by a solid background of cross-stitch.
Asterism	"**ASS**" tuh riz um	In jewelry, a term used for the starlike luminous figure seen in some rubies or sapphires.
Astragal	**AH** strah gull	In architecture, a small, semicircular molding.
Astylar	"a" "**STYLE**" ur	Without columns or pilasters.
Asuka	ah soo kah	A Japanese time period (538-645).
Ataujía	ah tah oo **HEE** ah	(Sp.) A term implying a metal surface inlaid with colored enamels, gold, or other metals.
Atelier	a tul **YAY**	(Fr.) An artist's or sculptor's studio.
Athénienne	a tay **NYEN**	(Fr.) A small stand or table on three legs.
Attelet	aht **LAY**	(Fr.) A small skewer made of silver or iron.
Atrium	"**A**" tree um	The central court of an ancient Roman house.
Aubergine	**OH** bur zheen	A purple glaze or enamel derived from manganese, used in Chinese ceramics.
Aubusson	**OH** buh soh(n)	The city of Aubusson in France, famous for its tapestry manufactories. Also, a generic term for types of carpets and tapestries.
Aula	"**AWE**" lah	In ancient Greek architecture, a court or hall.

Aulne Wood	ohn	A soft, reddish wood of the alder tree.
Aumund	ow moont	(Ger.) A faïence factory founded at Aumund in 1751.
Aurene Glass	**AW** reen	A term used for the iridescent glass developed at the Steuben Glass works by J. Carder; American, early 20th century.
Aureola	aw **REE** uh luh	An aureole.
Aureole	**OH** ree ole	A nimbus or halo emanating from the figure of a holy figure, as seen in Medieval and Renaissance art.
Aurillac Lace	oh ree **YAK**	A French lace of gold or silver thread.
Auvergne	oh **VAIRN**	A furniture style generally simple and massive, named for a former province in central France.
Aventail	**AV** un tale	In armor, the moveable front of a helmet.
Aventurine or Avanturine	uh **VENCH** uh reen uh **VAHNCH** uh reen	An opaque, brownish-colored glass flecked with fine, gold-colored particles.
Avignon	ah vee **NYOH(N)**	(Fr.) Pottery factories founded at Avignon in the late 16ᵗʰ century.
Avodiré Wood	a vuh duh **RAY**	A hard, light-colored wood of a West African tree.
Awaji Ware	ah wah jee	Japanese pottery made on the island of Awaji.

| Ayous Wood | ay **YOUS** | *A hard, white to pale-yellow wood of the Obeche, a tropical African tree.* |
| Azulejos | ah soo **LAY** <u>h</u>os | *(Sp.) Painted and glazed tiles made from red clay, used for decorating walls and floors.* |

B

Baccarat	**BAH** kuh rah	*Fine crystal glass manufactured at Baccarat, France from the 18th century to the present time.*
Bacchus	"**BACK**" us	*In ancient mythology, a god of wine and revelry. Also called Dionysus.*
Bachiru	bah chee loo	*A Japanese pick-like instrument used to carve ornamental designs on dyed ivory.*
Bacili Amatori	bah **CHEE** lee ah mah **TOH** ree	*(It.) Majolica emblematic love tokens.*
Bacini	bah **CHEE** nee	*(It.) Ornamental earthenware plaques, painted and glazed.*
Baguette	ba "**GET**"	*In jewelry, a rectangular shape given to a small gem. In architecture, a quarter- or half-round molding.*
Bahut	**BAH** hoot	*A medieval French coffer, originally small and portable. Has no fixed meaning today.*
Baigneuse	ben **YU(R)Z**	*A type of French upholstered daybed.*
Bakhshis	bahk shah yesh	*An oriental rug of Persian origin.*
Bakhtiari	bahk tee **AH** ree	*An oriental rug of Persian origin.*
Baku	bah koo	*An oriental rug of Caucasian origin.*

29

Balconet or Balconette	bal kuh "**NET**"	*In architecture, a low metal railing or balustrade before a window.*
Baldachin Baldaquin or Baldacchino	**BAWL** duh kin **BAWL** du keeno	*A canopy supported on columns over a throne or altar, used especially in medieval times.*
Baluchi	buh **LOO** chee	*Rugs of the nomadic and village- dwelling Beluch peoples of northeastern Iran.*
Baluchistan Beluchistan or Belouchistan	buh **LOO** chuh stan	*A term used for the rugs made by the Beluch people of Iran.*
Baluster	**BAL** us ter	*A small column supporting a rail.*
Bambocciata	bahm bo **CHA** tah	*In painting, depicting scenes from everyday, ordinary life.*
Banc	bahn(k)	*(Fr.) A bench, with or without a back.*
Bancelle	bah(n) **SELL**	*(Fr.) A small bench.*
Bancone	bahn **CO** nay	*(It.) A form of writing table.*
Bandwurm Glass	bahnt voorm	*(Ger.) A late 16th and 17th c. glass drinking vessel.*
Banquette	bang **KET** **BAN** kit bah(n) **KET**	*(Fr.) An upholstered seat or bench. Also, a sidewalk approximately 18" wide.*
Banuyo Wood	buh "**NEW**" yoe	*A hard, golden-brown or dark coffee-colored wood of a Philippine timber tree.*

Baphomets	**BA** fuh mets	In sculpture, curious stone figurines.
Baranovka	bah rah **NOHV** kah	A Polish porcelain factory founded at Baranovka, Volhynia in 1825.
Barbeaux	**BAR** boh	(Fr.) A term for 'cornflowers', used in connection with ceramic decoration.
Barberini	bahr beh **REE** nee	(It.) A tapestry factory founded at Rome in 1630. Also, a famous Roman glass vase.
Barbola Work	bahr **BOH** lah	The use of plastic paste ornaments as a decorative element on small articles made of wood or glass.
Barbotine	bahr buh **TEEN**	(Fr.) A term for early European ceramic ware with raised slip decoration.
Barbute	bahr **BOO** tay	(It.) A type of 15th c. helmet.
Bardiglio	bar **DEEL** yoh	(It.) A marble having a bluish or dark gray ground.
Bargello	bar "**JELLO**"	A type of needlework. Also called Hungarian stitch.
Barilla	buh **REEL** yuh	Ash obtained from a saltwork used in early glass-making.
Baroque	buh **ROKE**	A characteristic style of art and architecture of the 17th and 18th c. in Europe. The emphasis being on anything extravagantly ornate and exaggerated.
Barovier	ba roh **VeeAY**	A glass factory at Murano, Italy founded in the 19th c.

Basalt Ware	buh **SALT** **BA** salt **BAY** salt	(Eng.) The black stoneware introduced and made famous by Josiah Wedgwood in 1769.
Bas d'Armoire	bah dahr **MWAHR**	(Fr.) A low piece of furniture of commode size.
Basque	bahsk	A provincial furniture style named for a French province.
Basse-Taille	bahss-tie	(Fr.) A porcelain enamelling technique on a metal background carved in low relief.
Basset	bah **SAY**	(Fr.) A small table either round or square.
Basso-Rilievo	**BAH** soh-ree lee **EH** voh **BAH** so-ree "**LEAVE**" oh	(It. 'low relief') Relief sculpture.
Bateau-Lavoire, Groupe du	ba toh-lah **VWAHR**, "group" due	(Fr. 'the group of the floating wash house') An early 20th c. group of international artists located in Montmartre, Paris.
Bateau, Lit en	ba toh, lee ah(n)	(Fr.) A type of bed resembling the shape of a boat.
Batik	buh **TEEK** **BAD** ick	An Indonesian method of handprinting textiles by a form of resist-dyeing.
Baudekin	"**BAWDY**" kin	An embroidered fabric interwoven with gold or silver threads, primarily used for ceremonial robes.
Baudouine, Charles A.	boh doo **EEN**	A late 19th c. American cabinetmaker (1808-95).
Bauhaus	**BOW** "house"	A German school of architecture and industrial arts founded by Walter Gropius at Weimar in 1919.

Bayeux	bah **YUH(R)**	A French blonde lace made in Bayeux. Also, the Bayeux Tapestry made in the 11th century, considered one of the most famous pieces of historical needlework.
Bayreuth	bye royt	(Ger.) A ceramic factory founded at Bayreuth, Bavaria around 1713-14.
Beaujolais	**BO** zhuh **LAY**	A provincial furniture style named for a former French province.
Beauvais	bo **VAY**	(Fr.) A tapestry manufactory at Beauvais, France founded in 1664. Also, an active pottery center in and around Beauvais during the 14th to mid-16th century.
Beaux-Arts, École des	boze-"**R**", ay cole day	(Fr.) A Parisian school of fine arts founded in 1671.
Beeldekast	"**BALE**" duh cahst	(Dut.) A cupboard or wardrobe decorated with painted or carved figures.
Beinglas	bane glahs	(Ger.) A semi-opaque white glass produced in Bohemia and Thuringia from the late 18th -early 19th century.
Bellarmine	beller **MEEN** **BELLER** men	A German ceramic jug typically adorned with the figure of a bearded man.
Belleek	buh **LEEK**	A ceramic factory in County Fermanagh, Northern Ireland, established in 1863. The porcelain is famous for its thinness and iridescent glaze.
Belle Époque, La	bell ay **PUCK**, lah	(Fr.) 'The beautiful period' of art in France (1871-1914).

Bénitier	bay nee t^{ee}**YAY**	*(Fr.) A small container to hold holy water, usually of faïence or metal.*
Beni-ye	beh nee-yeh	*(Jap.) A two-colored print in pink and green.*
Benou Jaune	buh noo **ZHOHN**	*A type of mottled French marble.*
Berettino	berruh **TEE** no	*(It.) See Bianco Sopra Azzurro*
Bergama Rug *or* Bergamo	**BUR** guh muh bur **GAH** muh "**BEAR**" guh mo	*An oriental rug of Turkish origin.*
Bergère	behr **ZHAIR**	*(Fr.) An upholstered armchair with closed arms and loose seat cushion.*
Bertoia, Harry	bair **TOH** yah	*An American sculptor and furniture designer (1915-1978).*
Bésaque	bay **ZAK**	*A 15th century protective plate of armor designed to cover the armpits.*
Beshire Rug	bah sheer	*An oriental rug of Turkoman origin.*
Béton	bay **TOH(N)**	*(Fr.) Concrete.*
Bezel	**BEZ** ul	*In jewelry, that part of the ring, bracelet, etc., to which gems are attached.*
Bianco di Faenza	**BYAHN** coh dee fah **EN** tsa	*(It.) In ceramics, majolica having a thick white glaze. Introduced at Faenza in the 1540's.*
Bianco Sopra Azzurro	**BYAHN** coh **SO** prah ahd **DZOO** roh	*(It.) In ceramics, a term applied to a decorative technique executed in opaque white on a light or dark blue tin glaze ground.*

| Bianco Sopra Bianco | **BYAHN** coh **SO** prah **BYAHN** coh | *(It.) In ceramics, a term applied to a design executed in opaque white on a pale greyish or bluish white ground.* |

| Bibelot | **BEE** buh **LO** | *(Fr.) A small ornament or curio.* |

| Biberon | **BIB** uh rahn beeb **ROH**(**N**) | *(Fr.) A drinking vessel with an elongated spout.* |

| Bibliothèque | bee blee oh **TEK** | *(Fr.) A bookcase cabinet. Also, a library.* |

| Bidet | bee **DAY** | *(Fr.) A low basin-like bath.* |

| Bidri | **BID** ree | *A technique of inlay work used in India.* |

| Biedermeier | "**BEAD**" uh mire | *A term applied to a style of German art and furniture design prevalent from the 1820's through the 1850's.* |

| Bijar Rug | buh **JAR** **BEE** jar | *An oriental rug of Persian origin.* |

| Bijou | bee **ZHOO** | *(Fr.) A jewel or trinket.* |

| Bijouterie | bee zhoo "**TREE**" | *In jewelry, an article that is delicate, small, and exquisitely wrought. Composed mainly of gold and gemstones.* |

| Bilbao | bill **BAH** oh **BILL** boe uh | *A late 18th c. wall mirror.* |

| Billet | **BILL** it | *A term denoting the thumbpiece on a tankard. Also, molding used in Romanesque and Gothic architecture.* |

| Binche | bansh | *A Belgian lace from Flanders. Often used in costume trimming.* |

Bisette	bee **ZET**	(Fr.) A coarse, bobbin-made lace. Sometimes called peasant lace.
Bisque	bisk	(Fr.) Vitreous china that has not been glazed.
Bizen	bee zen	An early Japanese pottery center in the former province of Bizen. One of the six ancient kilns of Japan.
Blanc de Chine	blah(n) duh **SHEEN**	A fine white Chinese porcelain, first made at Tê Hua during the Ming period (1368-1643).
Blaue Reiter, Der	**BLOW** ur "writer", dur (rhymes with "now")	(Ger. 'the Blue Rider') A group of early 20th century artists who influenced the modern art movement.
Blaue Vier	**BLOW**ur veer (rhymes with "now")	(Ger. 'the Blue Four') Artists Klee, Kandinsy, Lyonel Feininger, and Alexei von Jawlensky who exhibited their work together in the 1920's.
Bleu-de-Roi	blu(r)-duh-**RWAH**	(Fr. 'king's blue') The blue enamel color found on Sèvres porcelain.
Bleu Persan	blu(r) "pair" **SAH(N)**	(Fr.) A name given to the blue-ground faïence of Nevers.
Bleu Turquin	blu(r) tur **CA(N)**	A type of marble from the Tuscany region.
Blonde de Caën	blohnd duh **CAH(N)**	Silk lace from Caën, France.
Bobêche	bo **BESH** bo **BASH**	(Fr.) A drip pan for a candlestick, lamp, or chandelier.
Bobéchon	boh bay **SHOH(N)**	(Fr.) A flat iron disc that is fitted with a bobêche.

Bocage	boh **KAHZH**	(Fr.) A decorative motif of leaves, foliage, flowers, etc., as used in a porcelain figure group or tapestry.
Boccaro Ware	**BOOK** uh roe **BAHK**	An early Chinese unglazed red stoneware manufactured in Yi-hsing.
Boehm, Edward M.	"beam"	An American ceramicist-sculptor who created the lifelike porcelain Boehm birds (1912-1969).
Bohemian Glass	boe **HEE** mee un	An ornamental glass character-ized by rich colors and engraved or incised patterns.
Bois de Rose	bwah duh **ROHZ**	(Fr.) Tulipwood.
Bois Durci	bwah dur **SEE**	In ornament, a wood-based plastic used to imitate ebony carvings.
Boiserie	bwah zuh **REE**	(Fr.) A term pertaining to woodwork; i.e., wood paneling, wainscoting, etc.
Bois Jourdain	bwah zhoor **DA(N)**	(Fr.) A type of marble with a dark gray ground.
Bois Noirci	bwah nwar **SEE**	(Fr.) An 18th c. term for wood stained to simulate ebony.
Boîte à Chandelles	bwaht ah shah(n) **DELL**	(Fr.) A box to hold candles.
Boîte à Farine	bwaht ah fah **REEN**	(Fr.) An open hanging flour box.
Boîte à Gaufre	bwaht ah **GOHFR**uh	(Fr.) A small wooden box used to hold honeycombs.
Boîte à Musique	bwaht ah mew **ZEEK**	(Fr.) A music box.
Boîte à Ouvrage	bwaht ah oo **VRAHZH**	(Fr.) A workbox.

Boîte à Sel	bwaht ah **SELL**	(Fr.) A small salt box.
Bokhara Rug	boh **KAH** ruh boo **KAH** ruh	An oriental rug of Turkoman origin.
Bombé	"bombay"	(Fr.) A convex or welling curve, as found in furniture.
Bonbonnière	bahn buh **NEAR** boh(n) bun **YAIR**	(Fr.) A small fancy box or dish for sweets.
Bonheur du Jour	"bun" ur due **ZHOOR**	(Fr.) A small 18th century lady's writing desk.
Bonnetière	bunt **YAIR**	(Fr.) A narrow wardrobe or cupboard with single door.
Bordeaux	"bore" "**DOE**"	(Fr.) A porcelain factory founded at Bordeaux in 1781.
Bori	boh lee	Japanese carvings on sword fittings.
Borne	"born"	(Fr.) A round or oval sofa having a central backrest.
Boteh-Miri	**BOH** tay-mee ree	A rug design consisting of leaves and flowers in a cluster.
Bottega	boe **TAY** guh boht **TEH** gah	(It.) A studio/shop of an artist.
Botticino	boht tee **CHEE** noh	(It.) Type of light and dark marbles.
Bouclé	boo **CLAY**	(Fr.) Yarn with loops; curled.
Boudeuse	boo **DURZ**	(Fr.) An upholstered salon seat.
Bouffioulx	boo "few"	Belgian stoneware made at Bouffioulx and other centers in the Walloon country from the late 16th century onward.
Bougeoir	boo **ZHWAHR**	(Fr.) A small candlestick.

Bougie Box	boo zhee	A small silver container used to hold a coil of wax taper.
Bouilloire	boo^{yuh} **WAHR**	(Fr.) A metal tea kettle mounted on a spirit burner.
Bouillotte	boo **YAHT** boo **YUT**	(Fr.) A type of 18th century table lamp. Also a small round card table of the 18th century.
Boulle or Buhl	bool	A decorative inlay on furniture using tortoiseshell and metals, practiced by French cabinet maker André Charles Boule (1642-1732).
Bout de Pied	boo duh **PYAY**	(Fr.) A term meaning end of foot section of a duchesse brisée or chaise longue.
Bowenite	**BOE** en ite	A mineral often mistaken for jade.
Braguette	bra "**GET**"	See Brayette
Brandegowkom	**BRAHN** duh "**HOW**" kohm	A silver bowl having two handles.
Bras de Cheminée	brah duh shuh mee **NAY**	(Fr.) Wall-sconces.
Bratina	**BRAH** tee nah	A Russian drinking vessel.
Brayette	bra **YET**	A front appendage to a suit of armor which protected the groin. Also, the breech of mail or skirt.
Brazier or Brasier	**BRAY** zher	A metal container for holding burning coals or charcoal.
Breccia	**BRECH** ee uh	A rock comprised of sharp - cornered fragments, usually embedded in sand, lime, or clay.

Breche Rose	bresh rohz	A type of mottled Italian marble.
Bresse	bress	A provincial furniture style named for a district in eastern France.
Bretagne	bruh **TAN** yuh	The French name for Brittany.
Bretesse	breh **TESS**	In medieval fortifications, a crenelated tower or bay of wood.
Breton	bret'n	A provincial furniture style named for an inhabitant of Brittany.
Breviary	**BREE** vee "err" ee	A book containing the daily prayers, hymns, and psalms said by the clergy at the canonical hours.
Bride Bouclée	breed boo **CLAY**	A French lace from Normandy, similar to Aleçon.
Bride Épinglée	breed ay pa(n) **GLAY**	A French lace from Normandy, similar to Aleçon.
Brides Ornées	breed or **NAY**	A French lace decorated with picots or pearls.
Bride Picotée	breed peek oh **TAY**	A French lace from Normandy.
Bride Tortillée	breed tor tee **YAY**	Aleçon lace from Normandy.
Brignoles	bree **NYOHL**	(Fr.) Type of marble with a yellowish-gold ground.
Briolette	bree oh "**LET**"	A teardrop diamond or other gem cut in triangular facets.
Brise-Soleil	"breeze"-soe **LAY**	(Fr.) A louvred sun-screen to reduce glare.
Brocade	broe **KAYD**	A fabric woven with an ornamental design in relief.

Brocatelle	brock uh **TELL**	*A heavy fabric with embossed figures.*
Broderie Anglaise	bro **DREE** ah(n) "**GLAZE**"	*An embroidery characterized by eyelet and artwork design.*
Broderie de Nancy	bro **DREE** duh nah(n) **SEE**	*A type of decorative needlework.*
Brücke, Die	"**BREW**"k^{ur}, dee	*(Ger. 'the bridge') An early 20th century group of expressionist artists.*
Brûle Parfum	brool pahr **FA**(**M**)	*(Fr.) A perfume burner.*
Brummagem	**BRUHM** uh jum	*An unrefined name for Birmingham, England. Also, cheap jewelry and articles manufactured there.*
Bucchero Ware	**BOOK** uh roe	*An ancient Etruscan blackware pottery.*
Bucranium	byoo **KRAY** nee um pl. -ah	*In classical architecture, an ornament in the form of an ox skull; e.g., on a frieze.*
Buen Retiro	bwen reh **TEE** roh	*An 18th century Spanish porcelain manufactory in the gardens of the royal palace near Madrid.*
Buffet	buh **FAY** boo **FAY**	*(Fr.) A sideboard or side table for display of tableware.*
Buffet à Deux Corps	...ah du(r) "**CORE**"	*(Fr.) A cupboard in two stages.*
Buffet à Glissants	...ah glee **SAH**(**N**)	*(Fr.) A low cupboard or credence with low recessed plateau and sliding end panels.*
Buffet Bas	...**BAH**	*(Fr.) A low panelled cupboard.*
Buffet Crédence	...kray **DAH**(**N**)**S**	*(Fr.) A low buffet, buffet à glissants, or buffet bas.*

Buffet-Vaisselier	...veh suh **LYAY**	*(Fr.) An open dresser above a lower enclosed cupboard.*
Buffneato	boof neh **AH** toh	*(It.) A type of marble with a buff-colored ground.*
Buhl	bool	*See Boulle.*
Buis Wood	bwee	*A very hard yellow wood of the box tree.*
Bunzlau	boon "slow"	*A pottery center founded at Bunzlau, Silesia during the Middle Ages, known for its distinctive salt-glazed stoneware.*
Burano	boo **RAH** no	*A Venetian lace from the Island of Burano.*
Bureau	byou **ROE**	*(Fr.) A writing table or desk. In America, a chest of drawers.*
Bureau à Caissona	...ah keh **SOHN** nah	*(Fr.) A kneehole writing desk.*
Bureau à Cylindre	...ah see **LA(N)** dr^{uh}	*(Fr.) A variety of a large cylinder-front desk.*
Bureau à Dos d'Âne	...ah doe **"DON"**	*(Fr.) A slant-front desk designed more for women.*
Bureau à Pente	...ah **PAH(N)T**	*(Fr.) A slant-front desk.*
Bureau Ministre	...mee **NEE** str^{uh}	*(Fr.) A kneehole writing table.*
Bureau Plat	...**PLAH**	*(Fr.) A large-sized writing table with a flat top.*
Burette	byou **RET**	*(Fr.) A cruet used especially for sacramental wine.*
Burgauté	bur go **TAY**	*An early Chinese ceramic technique employing mother-of-pearl and black lacquer. Also called Lac-Burgauté.*

Burgonet	bur go **NEH**	A lightweight open helmet worn in the 16th and 17th century.
Burujird Rug *or* Buriyerd	boh roo jaird	An oriental rug of Persian origin.
Buttenmann	boo tin mahn	(Ger.) A drinking vessel.
Byrnie *or* Byrne	"Bernie"	A body armor worn in the 10th century.
Byzantine	**BIZ** un teen **BIZ** un tine	As pertaining to the art and architecture of the Eastern Roman Empire or Byzantium.

C

Cabaret	ka buh **RAY**	A tea or coffee service, often including a small table or tray.
Cabasset	ka buh **SAY**	A helmet of the late 16th and 17th century.
Cabinet-Secrétaire de Cylindre	kah bee **NAY** -suh kray **TAIR** duh see **LA(N)** druh	(Fr.) A type of tall desk.
Cabistan Rug	**"CAB"** is tan	See Kabistan
Cabochon	**CAB** uh shahn	A precious stone polished but not cut into facets. In ornament, the cabochon motif (convex oval) was widely used during the 16th through 18th century.
Cabriole	**CAB** ree "ole"	Curved furniture legs, often resembling an animal's paw.
Cabriolet	**CAB** ree uh **LAY**	(Fr.) An 18th century small armchair having a concave back.
Cachepot	**CASH** "pot" **CASH** poe	(Fr.) An ornamental container used to hold or conceal a flowerpot.
Caduceus	kuh **DOO** see us kuh **DOO** syoos pl. -"sigh"	In mythology, the staff carried by Mercury or Hermes.
Caelatura	kah eh lah **TOO** rah	An art process executed in metal.
Caen	kah(n)	A late 18th century French porcelain manufactory.

Caffaggiolo	kah fah **JO** lo	*Italian majolica made in Caffaggiolo near Florence during the 16th century.*
Cailloutages	kah you **TAHZH**	*(Fr.) A term used for cream-colored earthenware.*
Caillouté	kah you **TAY**	*(Fr.) A form of gilded decoration used on Sèvres porcelain.*
Cairngorm	"care"n gorm	*A brown or yellow variety of crystalline quartz found among the Cairngorm mountains in Scotland.*
Caisson	keh **SOH(N)**	*(Fr.) A panel sunk into a coffered ceiling.*
Calambac Wood	**KA** lum back	*A hard brown wood, also called agalloch, from the east Indies.*
Calathus	**KAL** uh thos pl. -thoy	*See Kalathos*
Calcedony or Chalcedony	kal "**SAID**" uh nee **KAL** seh "**DOE**" knee	*A translucent variety of quartz, usually waxy or dull, and pale blue or grayish in color.*
Caliatour Wood	kah lee ah **TOUR**	*A very hard, bright red wood from the East Indies.*
Callot Figures	kah "**LOW**"	*The name used for grotesque figures of dwarfs, usually made of porcelain.*
Camagon Wood	kuh muh "**GONE**"	*A dark-colored hard wood from the Philippine Islands.*
Camaïeu, En	cah mah **YU(R)**, ah(n)	*(Fr.) The use of monochrome painting on pottery, porcelain, etc.*
Camail	kuh **MAIL**	*In armor, a 14th century guard of chain mail for the neck and shoulders.*

Cameo Habillé	...ah bee **YAY**	(Fr.) A carved cameo head of a person adorned with small gemstones.
Campagne	kah(m) **PAN** ʸᵘʰ	A lace worked with gold and colored silk threads, used to trim cloaks, buttons or scarves.
Campan	ka(m) **PAH(N)**	(Fr.) A group of marbles from the Hautes-Pyrénées, Campan district.
Campanile	"camp" uh "**KNEE**" lee kahm pah **NEE** leh	(It.) A bell tower often detached from the body of the church.
Campeche Wood	kahm **PEH** cheh	A very hard, brownish-red wood from Mexico.
Canadella	kah nah **DAY** yah	(Sp.) A type of glass ewer made in Catalonia.
Canapé	**CAN** uh "p" ka nuh **PAY**	(Fr.) A settee which was generally upholstered or caned.
Canapé à Corbeille	...ah core **BAY**	(Fr.) A settee with a characteristic horseshoe frame.
Canapé Dish	**CAN** nuh "p" ka nuh **PAY**	A covered silver entrée dish.
Cancelli	can **SEH** lee kahn **CHEH** lee	(It.) An ornamental barrier separating the sanctuary from the rest of the church.
Candaliere	kahn dahl **YAIR** ay	(It.) A style of grotesque ornamentation employed on Renaissance Italian majolica ware.
Canephora	kuh **NEF** uh ruh pl. -roy	An ornamental figure bearing a basket on his/her head.
Cannelé	can "**LAY**"	A silk fabric characterized by horizontal ribbing.

Cannelle Wood	kah **NELL**	A hard, white wood from the West Indies. Also called cinnamon bark.
Cannetille	can **TEE**^{yuh}	(Fr.) In jewelry, a filigree pattern of thin metal wires used as a decorative techique.
Canopic Jar	kuh **NO** pik	An ancient Egyptian jar used to contain the entrails of an embalmed body.
Cantagalli	cahn tah **GAH** lee	(It.) A ceramic manufactory founded at Florence in 1878 by Ulysses Cantagalli and known for its imitation majolica ware.
Cántaro	**KAHN** tah roh	(Sp.) A type of glass drinking vessel.
Cantharus	**KAN** thur us pl. -"rye"	See Kantharos
Cantilever	**CAN** tuh **LEE** ver	A projecting, bracket-like beam employed to support cornices, etc.
Cantir	kahn **TEER**	(Sp.) A type of 18th century glass vessel.
Cantonnière	kah(n) "ton" **YAIR**	(Fr.) A window or bed valance. Also, a French provincial corner armoire.
Capo di Monte	**KAH** poh dee **MON** tay	(It.) A porcelain factory founded at the royal palace of Capo de Monte in Naples in 1743.
Capriccio	kuh **PREE** choe / kuh **PREE** chee oh	A painting or print that contains bizarre or fantastic subjects.
Capucine	**KA** pyuh seen / ka pue **SEEN**	(Fr.) A term applied to wooden furniture used in the monastery rooms.

Caqueteuse or Caquetoire	kak **TU(R)Z** kak **TWAHR**	(Fr.) A type of armchair of 16th century design.
Carafe	kuh **RAF** ka **RAF**	(Fr.) A wide-mouthed glass or metal container used for beverages; a bottle without a stopper.
Caricature	**KAR** i kuh chur	A pictoral ridicule, exaggerating the physical characteristics of persons or things.
Carnelian or Cornelian	"car" **NEE** l'yun	A chalcedony that is flesh-red to brown-red in color.
Carolean	ka ruh **LEE** un	The furniture produced in the period of Charles I and II. (1645-1685)
Carolingian Art	"carol" **IN** jee un	The revival of the arts under the Emperor Charlemagne and his successors. (A.D. 8th-10th century)
Carquois, à la	"car" **KWAH** , ah lah	(Fr.) A painted ceramic decoration in the Rococo style.
Carrack	**KAR** ik	In porcelain, a term referring to the blue and white Chinese porcelain exported on ships known as carracks.
Carrara	kuh **RAH** ruh	A type of marble quarried at Carrara, Italy.
Carrickmacross	**KA** rik muh **CROSS**	An appliqué lace made near Carrickmacross, Ireland.
Cartel	"**CAR**" tell "car" **TELL**	(Fr.) A wall clock often made of bronze doré.
Cartellino	"car" teh **LEE** noh	In painting, the scroll bearing the name of the sponsor or artist.

Cartier, Inc.	"car" **TYAY**	(Fr.) A jewelry and silver establishment founded at Paris in 1847.
Cartisane	"car" tee **ZAHN**	A French lace or guipure, called parchment lace in England.
Cartonnier	"car" "ton" **YAY**	(Fr.) A filing cabinet or nest of boxes or cartons used independently or as an accessory to a piece of furniture.
Cartouche	car **TOOSH**	An ornamental motif resembling a scroll or tablet.
Caryatid	"**CARRY**" uh tid	A female figure used in place of a column as a decorative support.
Casque	"cask"	A medieval open helmet with a nose guard.
Cassapanca	kah suh **PAHN** kuh	An Italian Renaissance carved bench; a seat used as a chest.
Cassel	"castle"	(Ger.) A faïence factory from the late 17th century founded here. Also, a porcelain factory was established in 1766.
Cassolette	"**CASTLE**" let	(Fr.) An essence vase with pierced cover usually intended as a perfume burner.
Cassone	kuh **SO** nee kah **SO** nay	(It.) A large marriage chest.
Castel Durante	kah **STELL** doo **RAHN** tay	(It.) Umbrian majolica factories established at Castel Durante during the 16th century.
Castelli	kah **STELL** ee	(It.) A leading majolica center established here during the 17th and 18th century.

Caucasian Rugs	kaw **KAY** zhun	*Oriental rugs woven in Southern Russia between the Black and the Caspian Seas.*
Caudle Cup	**KAW** d'l	*A two-handled, deep drinking cup, usually having a cover.*
Caughley	"**COUGH**" lee	*An earthenware factory founded at Caughley, in Shropshire in 1750.*
Causeuse	koh **ZU(R)Z**	*(Fr.) A settee or love seat.*
Cavetto	kah **VET** toh	*(It.) A concave molding which is quarter-round.*
Cavo-Rilievo	**KAH** voh-ree **LEAVE** oh **KAH** voh-ree lee **EH** voh	*(It.) In sculpture, a form of hollow relief.*
Celadon	**SELL** uh dahn	*A Chinese porcelain or stoneware with a soft sea-green translucent glaze.*
Cella	"**SELL**" uh *pl.* -ee	*The central enclosed chamber of a classical temple.*
Cellarette or Cellaret	"**CELLAR**" et	*A receptacle fitted for wine bottles, usually made of wood.*
Cenacolo or Cenaculo	cheh **NAH** koh loh	*A painting depicting the Last Supper.*
Centaur	**SEN** "tar"	*A mythological being, half-man, half-horse.*
Cerberus	"**SIR**" buh rus	*In mythology, a triple-headed dog.*
Cerisier Wood	suh ree **ZYAY**	*A hard, reddish-veined wood from the cherry tree.*

Certosina	"chair" duh **SEEN** uh "chair" toh **ZEE** nah	*(It.) A 15ᵗʰ century technique of inlaying bone, wood, ivory, mother-of-pearl, etc. in geometric patterns on a dark ground.*
Ceruse	**SEER** oos si **ROOS**	*White lead; the basis of white oil-paint.*
Cesarea	**KIE** za ree	*see Kayseri*
Chaîne de Forçat	shen duh for **SAH**	*(Fr.) In jewelry, a type of Victorian gold chain.*
Chairs à la Capucin	ah lah ka "pew" **SA(N)**	*(Fr.) Rush-seated chairs.*
Chaise	shayz shez	*(Fr.) Chair*
Chaise à Accoudoir	...ah a kou **DWAHR**	*(Fr.) A form of chair with up-holstered and padded crestrail.*
Chaise à Bureau	...ah byou **ROE**	*(Fr.) A form of desk chair.*
Chaise à Capucine	...ah **KA** pyuh seen ...ah ka pue **SEEN**	*(Fr.) A type of side chair or open armchair having a rush or straw seat.*
Chaise à Vertugadin	...ah vair tue ga **DA(N)**	*(Fr.) A type of early small side chair.*
Chaise de Femme	...duh **FEM** ...duh **FAHM**	*(Fr.) A type of early armchair.*
Chaise de Paille	...duh **PAH** ʸᵘʰ	*(Fr.) A chair with a rush or straw seat.*
Chaise de Salle à Manger	...duh sal ah mah(n) **ZHAY**	*(Fr.) A dining room chair.*
Chaise Encoignure	...un **KAHN** yuhr ...ah(n) kwah **NYUR**	*(Fr.) A type of upholstered chair designed to be used in a corner.*

Chaise en Vis-à-Vis	...ah(n) vee-zah-vee	*(Fr.) A term applied to a conversation or straddle chair.*
Chaise Longue	..."long"	*(Fr.) A form of chair with an elongated seat and upholstered back.*
Chaise Percée	..."pair" **SAY**	*(Fr.) A caned-back chair with hinged seat used over a bathroom lavatory.*
Chaitya	**CHITE** yuh	*An Indian Buddhist sanctuary.*
Chalcedony	kal "**SAID**" ᵘʰ nee **KAL** seh "**DOE**" knee	*see Calcedony*
Chalcidicum	kal **CID** i "come" *pl.* -kuh	*An annex of an early Christian or Roman Basilica.*
Chamfered *or* Chamfer	**CHAM** furd	*In cabinetwork, a beveled or smoothed-off surface when edge has been cut away. Also, a small groove.*
Champlevé	shah(m) pluh **VAY**	*An enameling technique in which metal background is incised or hollowed out, filled with enamel and fired.*
Cha-no-yu	chah-noh-"you"	*Ceramic objects used in the Japanese tea ceremony.*
Chancellerie	shah(n) "sell" **REE**	*(Fr.) A type of tapestry having attributes of the Chancellor or Keeper of the Seats.*
Chantilly	shan "**TILL**" ee shah(n) tee **YEE**	*(Fr.) A pillow lace manufactured at Chantilly from the 17ᵗʰ century. Also, a porcelain factory founded here in 1725.*
Chantourné	shah(n) tour **NAY**	*(Fr.) A type of carved headboard found on Louis XIV period beds.*

Chaori	**KAH** oh ree	The porch of a temple in India.
Charpay	**CHAR** pay	(Turk.) A term of measurement pertaining to rugs.
Châsse	shahss	(Fr.) A case with hinged cover used for the relics of a saint.
Chassis	**CHAS** ee **SHAS** ee	In painting, the wooden framework to which the canvas is mounted. Also, the revolving stand where the armature is placed.
Chasuble	**CHAZ** uh bul	An ecclesiastical sleeveless outer vestment.
Châtaignier Wood	shah tay **NYAY**	A hard yellow white wood from the chestnut tree.
Château	sha **TOH**	(Fr.) A large country home.
Chatelaine	shad^{uh} "**LANE**"	An ornamental clasp or chain worn at the waist for suspending keys, scissors, trinkets, etc.
Chaton	sha **TOH(N)**	(Fr.) In jewelry, a term used for an imitation gem of paste, its pavilion backed with metal foil or silver. Also, the French term for a bezel.
Chatones	chah **TOH** ness	(Sp.) A term for ornamental nailheads used on furniture.
Chatoyant	shuh "**TOY**" unt	In jewelry, a term to describe a change in luster or color in certain gems; i.e., cat's eye.
Chauffe-Assiette	"show"f-a **SYET**	(Fr.) A plate warmer.

Chauffe-Linge	"show"f-**LA(N)ZH**	*(Fr.) A linen warmer.*
Chauffe-Lit	"show"f-**LEE**	*(Fr.) A bed warmer.*
Chauffe-Pieds	"show"f-**PYAY**	*(Fr.) A foot warmer.*
Chauffe-Plat	"show"f-**PLA**	*(Fr.) A unit over stove or fireplace for keeping food warm.*
Chauffeuse	"show" **FU(R)Z**	*(Fr.) A type of early fireside chair with a very low seat.*
Chausses	"show"ss	*A close fitting medieval armor of mail for the legs and feet.*
Chef d'Oeuvre	sheh **DU(R)V** ʳᵘʰ	*(Fr.) Masterpiece.*
Cheneau	shay "**NO**" shuh "**NO**"	*(Fr.) In architecture, a cresting above a cornice.*
Chenet	shuh **NEH**	*(Fr.) A term used for an andiron.*
Ch'êng Hua	chung wha	*(Ch.) A reign of the Ming dynasty (1465-89).*
Chêng Tê	jung tuh	*(Ch.) A reign of the Ming dynasty (1506-21).*
Chêng T'ung	jung tohng	*(Ch.) A reign of the Ming dynasty (1436-49).*
Chenille	shuh **NEEL**	*A velvety cord with short threads of silk or wood, having a protruding pile.*
Chequer	"**CHECK**" ur	*In decoration, a pattern of squares.*
Chê Shih	jur shur	*(Ch.) In painting, a brownish-colored earth pigment.*
Cheval	shuh **VAL**	*(Fr.) A full-length mirror on a frame. Also, a type of early English fire screen.*

Cheveret *or* Sheveret	**SHEV** uh ret	*A type of 18th century English small table.*
Chia	jeeah	*A Chinese ritual cup, sometimes having a cover.*
Chia Ching	jeeah jeeng	*(Ch.) A reign of the Ming dynasty (1522-66).*
Chia Ch'ing	jeeah cheeng	*(Ch.) A reign of the Ch'ing dynasty (1796-1820).*
Chiaroscuro	**KYAH** ruh **SKOO** roe kyah rohs **KOO** roh	*(It.) In drawing or painting, the technique of using strong emphasis on light and dark areas.*
Chi-Chao Tsun	jee-jow dsooen	*A Chinese water pot.*
Chichi *or* Tchichi	jee jee	*An oriental rug of Caucasian origin.*
Chi Chou Yao	jee "joe" yow	*A variety of Chinese ceramic ware.*
Ch'ien Lung	cheeen lohng	*(Ch.) A reign of the Ch'ing dynasty (1736-96).*
Chien Wên	jeeen "won"	*(Ch.) A reign of the Ming dynasty (1399-1402).*
Chien Yao	jeeen yow	*An early Chinese ceramic ware first made during the Sung dynasty (960-1279).*
Chiffonier	**SHIFF** uh **NEAR** "she" "fun" **YAY**	*(Fr.) A tall chest of drawers or bureau.*
Chiffonnière	shiff uh **NYAIR** "she" "fun" **YAIR**	*(Fr.) A small worktable generally used by ladies.*
Chifforobe	**SHIFF** uh "robe"	*A combination of chest of drawers and wardrobe.*

Chih	j^{uh}	A Chinese ritual drinking vessel.
Ch'ih Lung	ch^{uh} lohng	(Ch.) A form of dragon.
Chi Hung	jee hohng	Pertaining to Chinese ceramics, a term given to the red color derived from copper.
Ch'i-Lin	chee-leen	(Ch.) A mythical beast depicted in painting, ceramics and sculpture.
Chimera	kie **MEER** uh kuh keh	A mythical animal which takes numerous forms.
Chimere	shih "**MERE**" chih	A loose outer dress of a bishop.
Chiné	shee **NAY**	(Fr.) 18th century fabrics woven from silk threads dyed irregularly.
Ch'ing	cheeng	A Chinese dynasty (1644-1912).
Ch'ing Ho Hsien	cheeng huh sh^{ee}en	An early Chinese ceramic ware made at this location during the Sung dynasty (960-1279).
Ch'ing Pai	cheeng "by"	The Chinese name given to a bluish- or greenish-white glaze used on ceramics.
Ching T'ai	jeeng "tie"	(Ch.) A reign of the Ming dynasty (1450-57).
Ching tê Chên	jeeng tuh jun	An early Chinese ceramic center considered to be one of the finest in the world.
Chin Hu	jeen "who"	A Chinese wine ewer, usually pear-shaped with a long slender spout.

Chinikhana	"chin" ee **KAH** nah	A Hindustani term for an ornamental recess or niche.
Chinkinbori	cheen keen boh lee	(Jap.) A lacquer technique of rubbing gold in the incised design.
Chino	**CHEE** no	A strong twill cotton.
Chinoiserie	"she" nwahz **REE**	A European style of decorative work influenced by Chinese art.
Chintz	chints	A printed cotton fabric, usually glazed.
Chipolin	"she" poh **LA(N)**	(Fr.) An 18th century varnish technique simulating oriental lacquer.
Chiton	"**KITE**"n	In ancient Greece, the gown or tunic worn by both sexes.
Chiu	ch^{ee}oo	(Ch.) A bowl used for food, found in many variations of form.
Chopine	choe **PEEN** "**CHOP**" in	A high shoe or clog, worn in the 17th-18th century.
Chrismatory	**KRIZ** muh "tory"	A receptacle for the holy oils and chrism.
Chryselephantine	**KRIS** el uh **FAN** tin	Religious objects executed in ivory and gold.
Chrysoberyl	**KRIS** uh **BEH** rul	A semi-precious stone used in jewelry, generally in various shades of greenish-yellow or gold.
Chrysoprase	**KRIS** uh "**PRAISE**"	A semi-precious apple-green variety of chalcedony, much used in jewelry.
Christofle Silver, Inc.	kris "**TOUGH**"^{luh}	A French silver company founded at Paris in 1837, and noted for its silverplated flatware.

Chueh	j^{ue}eh	A Chinese ritual wine cup, ovoid-shaped, which stands on three legs.
Chü-Lü Hsien	jue-lue sh^{ee}en	An early Chinese ceramic ware made at this location during the Sung dynasty (960-1279).
Ch'ung Chêng	chohng jung	(Ch.) A reign of the Ming dynasty (1628-44).
Chün Yao or Kuan Chün Yao	j^{oo}een yow	An early Chinese ceramic ware made during the Sung dynasty in Honan province (960-1279).
Churrigueresque	**CHEW** ree guh **RESK**	A late 17th century Spanish baroque architectural style.
Chute	"shoot"	(Fr.) A long bronze or wood panel of relief decoration used on walls and furniture during the 17th -18th century
Ciborium	suh **BOE** ree um pl. -uh	A canopy supported by four columns, especially one covering an altar. Also, a covered ecclesiastical vessel for holding the reserved sacrament.
Cimarre	see **MAHR**	(Fr.) A ceremonial vessel, usually for wine.
Cincture	"**SINK**" chir	In architecture, a fillet encompassing a column.
Cinnabar	"**SIN**" uh bar	A native vermilion, used as a red pigment.
Cinquecento	**CHINK** wuh **CHEN** toe **CHEENK** way	Pertaining to the Italian art period 1500-1600.
Cinquefoil	**SINK** foil **SANK**	(Fr.) A decorative motif using a five-cusped or five-leaved pattern.

Cipolin	**SIP** uh lin	An impure variety of white marble.
Circassian	sir **CASH** un	An oriental rug of Caucasian origin. Also a brown and striped walnut wood from the Russian Black Sea area, as well as black-veined wood of the English walnut.
Ciré	si **RAY** see	(Fr.) A polished, highly glazed finish for fabrics.
Cire Perdue	seer "pair" **DUE**	(Fr.) A term for the lost-wax process of casting metal sculpture and jewelry.
Ciselé Velvet	**"SEIZE"** uh **LAY** **"SEIZE" LAY**	(Fr.) A term applied to various types of cut silk velvet.
Ciseleur	"seize" **LUR**	A metal engraver.
Cistercian Ware	si **STIR** shun	A 16th century English red pottery.
Citronnier Wood	si trun **NYAY**	A firm white-veined wood of the citron tree of Asia and Middle Europe.
Classeur	klah **SUHR**	(Fr.) A small open case.
Clepsydra	**KLEP** suh druh	An ancient water-clock.
Cliché	klee **SHAY**	(Fr.) A relief in metal by a process of electroplating, from which engravings are printed.
Cliché-Verre	klee shay-**VAIR**	(Fr.) A type of photographic print.
Clichy Glasshouse	klee **SHEE**	(Fr.) A glass factory founded at Clichy in 1840, famous for its paperweights.
Clignancourt	"clean" yah(n) **COOR**	(Fr.) A porcelain factory founded at Clignancourt, Paris in 1771.

Clochette	kluh **SHET**	(Fr.) A small bell-shaped ornament.
Cloisonné	cloy z'n **AY** clwah zun **NAY**	A technique of enamel decoration in which color areas are separated by metal lines.
Coade Stone	"code"	A late 19th century ceramic imitation of stonework popular in England.
Cochineal	**KAHCH** uh neel	A natural red dye of insect origin.
Cockatrice	**COCK** uh tris	A mythological monster, half-cock, half-dragon.
Coelanaglyphic	see **LAN** uh **GLIF** ic	In sculpture, a hollow relief.
Coffre	**KAW** fur kohf[ruh]	A type of early French chest.
Coiffeuse	kwah **FU(R)Z**	(Fr.) A dressing table.
Colcothar	**KAHL** kuh thur	A red oxide pigment, now obsolete.
Collage	kuh **LAHZH**	A composition of objects and/or materials glued to a canvas or panel.
Colichemarde	ko leesh **MARD**	A 17th century small sword.
Cologne	kuh **LONE**	An early center of Rhenish stoneware at Cologne, Germany. The most active pottery was in the Maximinenstrasse.
Colophon	**KAH** luh "fun"	In printing, the device or inscription giving information (title, printer's name, date of publication, etc.)
Comblanchien	koh(m) blah(n) shya(n)	(Fr.) A rose-colored limestone, quarried in southern France.

Commedia dell'Arte	kuh "**MAID**" ee uh del "**LARD**" ee *or* kohm **MED** yah dell **AHR** teh	*(It.) The medieval Italian comedy group who inspired European literary and art circles.*
Commode	kuh **MODE** kuh "**MUD**"	*(Fr.) An 18th century low chest of drawers, usually with a marble top.*
Commode-Desserte	kuh **MODE**-day **SAIRT**	*(Fr.) A type of commode with open-shelf case.*
Compagnie des Indes	ko(m) pan **YEE** day **ZA(N)D**	*A generic term for the early Chinese porcelain produced and exported to Europe and America.*
Console Table	**KAHN** sole	*A table supported by ornamental brackets or consoles. Also, a small table placed against a wall with legs in the form of consoles.*
Contrepartie	koh(n) tr^uh par **TEE**	*A marquetry technique.*
Copaïba Wood	ko **PIE** buh ko **PAY** buh	*A hard, red-spotted wood of the Copaïba tree of Brazil.*
Coque de Perle	cuck duh **PAIRL**	*(Fr.) A term for a pearl shell.*
Coquerelles	cuck **RELL**	*(Fr.) A heraldric term denoting a bunch of three filberts in their husks.*
Coquillage	ko keh **LAHZH** coh "key" **YAHZH**	*In ornament, a term applied in cabinetwork to decoration imitating the shell motif.*
Coquilla	coh "**KEY**" yah	*The coquilla nut of South America employed for carving.*
Coquille	koe **KEEL** coh "**KEY**"^yuh	*An illustration board whose surface has an embossed texture.*
Coquina	koe "**KEY**" nuh	*A building stone of broken shells and coral cemented together.*

C

Corail Wood	kuh **RAIL** koh **RAIL**	A soft, fiery red-veined wood of the coral tree of the East and West Indies.
Corbel	**CORE** bul	A projecting architectural bracket which supports a weight.
Cordelière	core duh **LYAIR**	(Fr.) A mid-19th century long beaded girdle.
Cordonnet	core duh **NAY**	In lace making, the outline of a lace motif using cord, thread or yarn, giving it sharper definition.
Corinthian	core **IN** thee un	The Greek order of architecture characterized by a slender, fluted column and capital, decorated with acanthus leaves.
Cormier Wood	core "me" **AY**	A hard reddish wood of the service tree.
Corne, à la	corn, ah lah	(Fr.) An 18th century polychrome ceramic decoration using motifs of flowers, bees, butterflies, etc.
Cornucopia	corn uh **KOE** "pea" uh	A decorative motif represented as a horn overflowing with fruits, flowers and grain.
Coromandel	**CAR** uh **MAN** dul	A brightly colored lacquer work characterized by an incised design. Also, a hard, brownish wood of an Asian tree.
Corselet	"**CORE**" slit	A 16th century suit of half or three-quarter armor.
Corundum	kuh **RUN** dum	A precious stone, notable for being hard and transparent.

Cosmati Work	kahz **MAH** dee koz **MAH** dee	(It.) A medieval architectural decoration in mosaic and marble inlay work.
Cotière	koht **YAIR**	(Fr.) A late Renaissance long chain with pendant, often elaborate.
Couche	coosh	(Fr.) A term for couch or bed.
Coudières	"coo" **DYAIR**	(Fr.) In medieval armor, elbow-plates.
Coupe	coop	A Chinese ceramic receptacle that held water for cleaning brushes.
Courbaril Wood	**KER** buh ril	A hard, pale red-veined wood of the locust tree of Asia and America.
Couronné	"coo" "run" **AY**	(Fr.) In lace making, the small loops edging the cordonnet.
Couter	"**COO**" ter	A medieval protective piece of armor for the elbow.
Craquelle	kra **KELL**	A rough-textured art glass.
Craquelure	"crack" "**LURE**"	(Fr.) The network of fine cracks found on the surface of old oil paintings.
Crèche Art	kresh kraysh	(Fr.) A reconstruction of the Nativity Scene.
Crédence	kray **DAH(N)S**	(Fr.) An early sideboard or buffet.
Credenza	kruh **DENZ** uh kree **DENZ** uh kreh **DENT** sah	(It.) A sideboard or buffet.

Credenzina	kruh denz **EE** nah kreh dent **SEE** nah	*(It.) A small credenza.*
Creese or Kris	"crease"	*A typical Malay short sword or dagger.*
Creil	krel	*(Fr.) A ceramic factory founded at Creil, Oise in 1794.*
Crenel or Crenelle	**KREN** ul kri **NELL**	*In architecture, the open spaces between the merlons of a battlement.*
Créquier	kray kee **AY**	*(Fr.) A heraldic term applied to a chandelier of seven branches.*
Crespine	kruh **SPEEN**	*(Fr.) In medieval armor, a headdress.*
Cresset	**KRIS** it	*A medieval metal container for holding burning oil, wood, etc., and mounted as a torch or lantern.*
Cretonne	**KREE** tahn kri "**TON**"	*A decorative fabric with colorfully printed patterns.*
Crevé	kruh **VAY**	*(Fr.) In etching, a defect on the plate caused by over-biting.*
Criblé	kree **BLAY**	*(Fr.) A technique of decorating wood and metal surfaces by means of punching dots to create an image. Also called Manière Criblée.*
Crinet	**KRIN** it	*Medieval armor plates protecting the upper surface of a horse's neck.*
Criseby	kreeze bee	*(Ger.) A faïence factory founded at Criseby in 1759.*

Criosphinx	"cry" "o" sfinks	A sphinx figure having the head of a ram.
Crochet	kro **SHAY**	A form of lace worked with a one-hooked needle.
Cromlech	**KRAHM** lek	Prehistoric circular monuments.
Croquis	kroh "**KEY**"	(Fr.) A preliminary sketch or drawing.
Crozier or Crosier	"**CROW**" zhur	The pastoral staff of a bishop or abbot used as a symbol of his function.
Crustae	**CRUS** "tea" pl. -tie	A term used for the repoussé metal plaques which decorated Roman cups or vases.
Crystallo-Céramie	kree stah loh- "say" rah **MEE**	(Fr.) The molded porcelain relief figures within crystal glass (often a paperweight).
Cubitiere	"cue" buh "**TIRE**"	A protective steel plate elbow guard in medieval armor.
Cuenca	**KWEN** kah	(Sp.) An early decorating technique used on pottery tiles.
Cuerda Seca	**KWAIR** duh "**SAKE**" uh **KWAIR** thah **SEH** kah	(Sp.) An early decorating technique used on pottery tiles and dishes.
Cuirass	kwee **RASS**	A close-fitting armor covering the body from neck to girdle, originally made of leather. Also, the breastplate of such armor.
Cuirasse Esthétique	kwee rass es tay **TEEK**	(Fr.) A popular style of armor for high Renaissance and Mannerist period history paintings.

Cuir-Bouilli	"queer"-boo **YEE**	(Fr.) Leather molded and shaped into various forms.
Cuir Ciselé	"queer" "seize" **LAY**	(Fr.) A technique of decorating leather by means of cutting a design on the surface.
Cuisse or Cuish	kwis kwish	A medieval defensive plate armor used for protection of the thigh.
Culet	"**CUE**" lit	In jewelry, a small facet at the base of a gem.
Cupola	"**CUE**" puh luh	In architecture, a dome; a concave roof of a building.
Curragh Lace or Currach	**KUR** ruh **KUR** ruck	An imitation of the lace patterns of Brussels. Also called Irish point.
Curricle	**KUR** i kul	A style of armchair resembling the lines of an open carriage.
Curule	"**CUE**" "rule"	A variety of an x-shaped stool with no back.
Cyathus	"**SIGH**" uh thus pl. -"thigh"	An ancient Greek ladle used for filling drinking cups with wine. Also called Kyathos.
Cycladic	si "**CLAD**" ik	Pertaining to the Bronze Age art and civilization of the Cyclades (c. 3000 -1100 B.C.).
Cylix or Kylix	"**SIGH**" lix pl. **SILL** uh keez **KIE** lix pl. **KILL** uh keez	A wide, shallow cup with horizontal handles and tall stem.
Cyma Curve	"**SIGH**" muh	A molding, the profile of which is a continuous double curve.

Cymaise	"sea" **MEZ**	*An early pewter wine vessel.*
Cymatium	si **MAY** shee um *pl.* -uh	*In classical architecture, the uppermost member of a cornice.*
Cytise Wood	"sea" **"TEASE"**	*A very hard greenish wood of the cystisus shrub. Also called Ébénier des Alpes.*
Cyzicenus	siz ee **SEE** nus	*In ancient architecture, a large chamber decorated with sculpture.*

C

D

Dada	**DAH** dah	An early 20th century anti-art movement originating in Zurich, Switzerland, expressing outrage at world conditions.
Dado	"**DAY**" "doe"	In architecture, the central part of a pedestal.
Daedalid	**DED**'l id **DEED**'l id	Pertaining to a style of terra-cotta Greek sculpture during the 7th century B.C. Also, a type of vase painting.
Daedalus	**DED** uh lus	(Gk.) A mythological figure personifying the beginning of the arts of sculpture and architecture.
Daghestan	**DAG** uh **STAN** **DAHG** uh **STAHN**	An oriental rug of Caucasian origin.
Daimyo Nanako	dah ee myoh nah nah koh	(Jap.) A type of surface decoration on Japanese sword mountings.
Dais	"**DAY**" iss "**DIE**" iss	A raised platform.
Dai-Sho	dah ee-"show"	The long and short swords carried by Japanese military men.
Dai-Sho-No-Soroimono	dah ee-"show"-noh-"solo" ee moh noh	(Jap.) The complete set of fittings for a pair of swords.
Damascening	**DAM** uh "**SEEN**" ing	Process of decorating metals to produce a watered pattern. Also, a technique of encrusting precious metals on a steel surface.

Damask	**DAM** usk	A reversible rich fabric woven with patterns.
Daum Frères	dome frair	(Fr.) A glassmaking factory founded at Nancy in 1875.
Dauphiné	"doe" fee **NAY**	A provincial style of furniture, named for a former French province.
Décollage	"day" cul **LAHZH**	A method of tearing away parts of paper layers to create an image.
Décor Bois	"day" "core" **BWAH**	Trompe l'oeil painted decorations on ceramics simulating grained wood.
Découpage	"day" coo **PAHZH**	The art of decorating with paper cutouts or other flat materials and then varnished.
De Distel	duh **DIS** tul	(Dut.) An earthenware factory at Amsterdam during the late 19th and early 20th century.
Deesis or Deisis	dee **EE** sis	A depiction of Christ enthroned and flanked by the Virgin Mary and John the Baptist.
Delft	delft	A tin-glazed Dutch earthenware, decorated with cobalt blue.
Della Robbia	**DELL** ah "**ROE**" bee ah	An early tin-glazed terra-cotta made by a Florentine Renaissance family of sculptors.
Demi Grand Feu	duh mee grah(n) **FU(R)**	(Fr.) Pertaining to medium fired glazes used on ceramics.
Demirdji	dah meer chee dem **UR** gee	An oriental rug of Turkish origin.

D

Demoiselle à Atourner	duh mwah **ZELL** ah ah tour **NAY**	*(Fr.) An early form of wig stand.*
Dentelle	dah(n) **TELL**	*(Fr.) A term referring to lace or lace-work.*
Dentelle à la Vierge	dah(n) tell ah lah **VYAIRZH**	*(Fr.) A peasant lace with a double ground from Normandy.*
Déposé	day poh **ZAY**	*(Fr.) A term used to denote a patent or copyright.*
Derbend Rug	**DUR** bend	*An oriental rug of Caucasian origin.*
Deruta	"day" **"RUDE"** uh deh **ROO** tah	*(It.) A pottery center at Deruta, Umbria founded in the late 15th century, known for its painted majolica ware.*
Deshilado	deh see **LAH** thoe	*(Sp.) A linen work with cut and drawn thread.*
Desserte	"day" **SAIRT**	*(Fr.) A side table or dumb-waiter.*
Dessus de Porte	duh sue duh **"PORT"**	*(Fr.) A horizontal painting designed specifically for use over a doorway.*
De Stijl	duh **STA**eel	*A Dutch art movement originating during the First World War.*
Deutsche Blumen	**DOYT** shuh **BLOOM** en	*(Ger.) A term for flowers painted naturalistically on ceramics.*
Deutsche Werkstätten	**DOYT** shuh **VAIRK** shta t'n	*A German art organization founded in the late 19th century.*
Deutscher Werkbund	**DOYT** shuh **VAIRK** boond	*A German association of man-ufacturers and architects founded in the early 20th century.*

Dhurri Rug *or* Dhurrie, Durrie	**DUR** ree **DAR** ree	A flat-woven, nonpile cotton rug of India.
Diablerie	dee **AH** bluh ree	In art, an infernal scene; dealings with the devil.
Diadem	"**DYE**" uh dem	A crown or ornamental headband.
Diamanté	dyah mah(n) **TAY**	(Fr.) A type of colorless paste.
Dimity	"**DIM**" i tee	A light cotton fabric.
Dinanderie	dee nah(n) **DREE**	An early brassware made in and around the Belgian town of Dinant. Also, a term applied to articles of brass made elsewhere.
Dionysus	"die" uh **NIE** sus	In classical mythology, the god of wine and revelry. Also called Bacchus.
Diorama	"die" uh "**RAM**" uh "die" uh **RAH** muh	A three-dimensional representation of a scene, often in miniature.
Diptych	**DIP** tik	A hinged pair of panels or leaves.
Directoire	dee rek **TWAHR**	(Fr.) A decorative arts style of the late 18th century.
Disegno	dee **SEN** yoh	(It.) A term for design or drawing.
Dis-torba	dis-**TOR** bah	(Turk.) A small bag used for storage.
Divan	"**DYE**" van duh **VAN**	A long, cushioned seat or couch, usually without arms or back.
Djidjim Rug *or* Djijim	jah ah jeem **JEH** jum	A term applied to various flat weaves. Also, a type of embroidered hand-woven rug.

D

Djushaghan Rug	joh sheh gahn	*See Joshaghan*
Doccia	**DOE** chuh **DOH** chah	*(It.) A porcelain factory founded near Florence in the 18th century.*
Doppelwandglas	**DOE** puhl **VAHND GLAHS**	*(Ger.) A decorative art process on glass using gold and/or silver leaf.*
Dopskal	"dope" skole	*(Swe.) A small drinking vessel, usually made of silver.*
Doric	**DOOR** ik	*In architecture, the oldest and plainest of the three Greek orders.*
Dorotheenthal	**DOE** roe **TAY**en tahl	*(Ger.) A faïence factory founded at Dorotheenthal near Arnstadt in Thuringia in 1715.*
Dossal or Dossel	**DAH** sul	*An ornamental hanging cloth placed at the back of the altar.*
Dossier	**DOE** syay	*(Fr.) A term applied to the headboard and footboard of a bed or chair back.*
Douai	doo **AY**	*(Fr.) A factory founded at Douai, Nord in 1781, for making faïence fine.*
Doughty, Susan Dorothy	**DOW** tee	*An English ceramist known for her ceramic birds (1892-1962).*
Dozar	**DOE** zar	*An Iranian term used in rug measurement.*
Drap d'Or	drah "**DOOR**"	*(Fr.) A term applied to gold cloth.*
Draperie Mouillée	drah pree moo **YAY**	*(Fr.) In figure sculpture, a thin drapery revealing the form beneath.*

D

Dreihausen	"dry" howz^{un}	(Ger.) A term applied to a small group of early stoneware vessels having stamped ornamentation.
Dressoir	dreh **SWAHR**	(Fr.) A sideboard or dresser.
Drollery or Drôlerie	**DROE** luh ree drohl **REE**	In art, a humorous picture.
Droschel	**DROH** sh'l	(Flem.) In lace-making, pertaining to handmade bobbin net.
Dryad	"**DRY**" ud pl. -deez	In mythology, a nymph of the woods.
Duchesse	due **SHESS**	(Fr.) A type of chaise longue characterized by chair-form ends.
Duchesse Brisée	due **SHESS** bree **ZAY**	(Fr.) A chaise longue made in two or three pieces.
Duchesse Lace	due **SHESS**	A type of 19th century Brussels bobbin lace resembling the guipure de Flandres made at Bruges.
Duecento	doo uh **CHEN** toe	Pertaining to the Italian art period 1200-1300.
Dumortierite	doo "**MORE**" tee uh **RIT**	A type of gemstone.
Duomo	**DWOE** moe	(It.) A cathedral.
Durlach	dur la<u>h</u>	(Ger.) A faïence factory at Durlach Baden, founded in 1723.
Duvet	due **VAY**	A quilt, usually with a removable cover.

E

Eau-forte	"o"-"fort"	*(Fr.) A term frequently used as a synonym for etching.*
Ébauche	ay **BOHSH**	*In oil painting, a rough sketch; the first underpainting.*
Ébénier des Alpes	ay bay **NYAY** day **ZALP**	*See Cytise Wood*
Ébéniste	ay bay **NEEST**	*(Fr.) A cabinetmaker whose specialty is veneered furniture.*
Ébénisterie	ay bay nees **TREE**	*(Fr.) A term meaning cabinetmaking; displaying the work of the cabinetmaker.*
Échelle	ay "**SHELL**"	*(Fr.) In jewelry, a set of graduated dress ornaments.*
Echinus	uh **KIE** nus *pl.* -"nigh"	*An ovolo molding. Also, the circular molding below the abacus of a Doric column.*
Échoppe	ay **SHUP**	*(Fr.) An etching and engraving needle whose point is beveled to an oval facet.*
Eckernförde	**EK** kairn **FURD**uh	*(Ger.) A faïence factory founded at Eckernförde, Schleswig in 1765.*
Eclecticism	eh **KLEK** tuh **SIZ** um	*A tendency in the arts to combine various styles from other art movements.*

Écorché	ay "core" **SHAY**	*(Fr.) A picture or statuette of a human form or animal where skin is stripped off to show the muscular construction.*
Écran	ay **KRAH(N)**	*(Fr.) A fire screen.*
Écran à Coulisse	...ah "coo" **"LEASE"**	*(Fr.) A type of fire screen with panel sliding in grooves.*
Écran à Éclisse	...ah ay **KLEESS**	*(Fr.) A pole screen of tripod form.*
Écran à Éventail	...ah ay vah(n) **"TIE"**	*(Fr.) A bronze doré fan-shaped fire screen.*
Écran Pupitre	...pue **PEE**truh	*(Fr.) A writing desk with fitted screen.*
Écrin	ay **KRA(N)**	*(Fr.) A jewel case.*
Écritoire	ay kree **TWAHR**	*(Fr.) An inkstand or compartment fitted for pen and ink.*
Écru	ay **"CREW"**	*(Fr.) A light tan color as raw silk or unbleached linen.*
Ectype	**EK** "type"	*A reproduction of an original.*
Écuelle	ay "cue" **ELL**	*(Fr.) A porringer made of silver, faïence, or porcelain.*
Edo	**EH** doe	*(Jap.) An historical period (1615-1867).*
Églomisé	ay "glow" mee **ZAY**	*(Fr.) The process of decorating glass by painting or drawing on the underside, then backing it with metal foil.*
Égouttoir	ay goo **TWAHR**	*(Fr.) A plate rack.*
Eilat Stone	ay **LAHT**	*A type of opaque mineral, used in jewelry.*

Eiraku Ware	eh ee rah koo	(Jap.) A variety of porcelain made in Kyoto.
Eleusinian	el "you" **SIN** ee un	A black marble from Greece.
Émail	ay "my" ay **MAH**yuh	
Émail en Blanc	...ah(n) **BLAH(N)**	(Fr.) A white enamel.
Émail en Résille Sur Verre	...ah(n) ray **ZEE**yuh sur **VAIR**	(Fr.) A decorative enamel process on glass.
Émail en Ronde Bosse	...ah(n) roh(n)d "bus"	(Fr.) A decorative enamel process on an object in the round.
Émail Ombrant	...oh(m) **BRAH(N)**	(Fr.) A decorative technique on pottery using colored glazes over incised motifs.
Emaux de Basse-Tailleay	moe duh bahs-**TIE**	(Fr.) A technique of enameling on sunken relief.
Emaux de Niellure	"a" moe duh nyay **"LURE"**	(Fr.) Deeply cut lines in metal, filled with enamels resembling niello.
Embu	ah(m) **BUE**	(Fr.) In oil painting, the dull area on the surface, caused by the colors sinking in.
Empaistic	em **"PACE"** tik	An early decorative practice of inlaying metal in metal.
Empaquetage	ah(m) "pack" **TAHZH**	A type of art form consisting of wrapping objects with common materials such as plastic sheeting.
Encaustic	in **"CAUSTIC"**	In painting, a technique mixing hot wax in with pigments.
Enceinte	en **"SAINT"** ah(n) **SA(N)T**	(Fr.) The continuous wall around the city or castle.

Encoignure	in "**CON**" yur in "**COIN**" yur ah(n) cun **YUR**	(Fr.) A low corner cabinet, buffet or cupboard, made to fit into a corner.
Encoignure à Deux Corps	...ah du(r) "**CORE**"	(Fr.) A type of tall cupboard made in two sections.
En Esclavage	ahn "s" clah **VAHZH**	(Fr.) A necklace of three chains which hang approximately equidistant from each other.
Enfilade	ah(n) fee **LAHD**	(Fr.) A low buffet with four or more cupboard doors. Also, the alignment of doors on an axis, that extends through a series of rooms.
Enghalskrug	ehnk hahlz kroog	(Ger.) A type of long-necked faïence jug.
Enghien Tapestries	en h(y)en	A 16th century weaving center at Enghien, Belgium.
Engobe	**AHN** gobe ah(n) **GOBE**	(Fr.) A type of clay (slip) applied over pottery to hide its natural color.
Engrêlure	ah(n) "gray" "**LURE**"	(Fr.) A lace making term for one of two edges of lace, the other being couronné.
Enile Rug	eh nee **LEH**	An oriental rug of Anatolian classification. A type of modern Oushak.
Enneastyle	"**N**" ee uh "still"	A portico having nine columns in a row.
Entasis	"**N**" tuh sis	The slight convex curvature given to a column or spire.
Entrée Dish	**AHN** tray	A covered dish to hold food, usually made of silver.

Entre-fenêtre	ah(n)^{truh}-fuh **NET**^{ruh}	(Fr.) A narrow tapestry panel, usually hung between windows.
Entrelacs	ah(n)^{truh} **LAH**	A decorative border of intertwining lines and curves.
Epaulet	**EP** uh let ep uh **LET**	Ornamental shoulder-pieces worn on uniforms.
Épaulette	ay poh **LET**	See Epaulet
Épaulière	ay "pole" **YAIR**	(Fr.) In armor, medieval shoulder plates.
Epergne	i **PURN** ee- ay-	An ornamental centerpiece for a table.
Epi	ay **PEE**	(Fr.) The topmost point; i.e., a spire.
Epigone	**EP** i "go"n	An imitator or follower of an important artist, etc.
Epinaos	ay pee **NAY** ohs eh pee **NAH** ohs	(Gk.) A space in the rear of the cella of an ancient Greek temple.
Épine-Vinette Wood	ay peen-vee **NET**	(Fr.) A hard yellow wood of the hawthorne tree.
Éponge, Boîte à	ay **PU(N)ZH**, bwaht ah	(Fr.) A silver sponge box.
Épreuve d'Artiste	ay pru(r)v dahr **TEEST**	(Fr. 'artist's proof') In printing, the first impression kept by the artist.
Érable Wood	ay **RAH** bl^{uh}	(Fr.) A hard reddish-veined, wavy wood of the maple tree.
Erfurt Pottery	air foort	(Ger.) A faïence factory in Erfurt, Thuringia, founded in 1717.

Escabeau	"s" kah **BOE**	*(Fr.) An early type of joined stool.*
Esclavage	"s" klah **VAHZH**	*see En Esclavage*
Escritoire	"**S**" kruh twahr	*A term applied to types of English writing furniture.*
Escudella ab Orelles	"s" "coo" **DAY** yah ahb oh **RAY** "yes"	*(Sp.) A type of 15th and 16th century ceramic bowl from Valencia, characterized by handles.*
Escudié	"s" "coo" **DYAY**	*(Fr.) A buffet-vaisselier, called escrudié in Gascogne.*
Escutcheon	uh **SKUH** chun	*In heraldry, a shield with a coat of arms. Also, the metal plate used to protect a key-hole.*
Espagnolette	eh spa nyuh **LET**	*A decorative bronze bust of a female head found on French Rococo furniture.*
Esparto	i **SPAHR** toe	*A coarse grass used for making paper.*
Espetera	eh speh **TEH** rah	*(Sp.) A wrought iron plaque used for hanging utensils.*
Esquisse	es **KEES**	*(Fr.) A preliminary outline for a painting or sculpture.*
Estagnié	es tan **YAY**	*(Fr.) A type of hanging or standing open shelf for displaying pewter.*
Estampille	es tah(m) **PEE**yuh	*(Fr.) A maker's mark stamped on a piece of French furniture.*
Estoc	eh **STAHK**	*In arms, a thrusting sword with a long, narrow, quadrangular blade used during the 13th through 17th century.*

Étagère	ay tah **ZHAIR**	(Fr.) Open shelves, either free-standing or hanging.
Étimier	ay tee **MYAY**	(Fr.) A type of simple cupboard or double-bodied buffet.
Etruscan	i **TRUSS** kun	A style of interior design based on the architecture, ornament and furniture of the ancient Etruscans.
Étui	ay **TWEE**	(Fr.) A small box or decorative case.
Eulenkrug	"**OIL**" en **KROOG**	(Ger.) A type of earthenware jug shaped like an owl.
Eurythmy or Eurhythmy	"you" **RI**T**H** mee	In architecture, a term to describe a harmoniously ordered or proportioned relationship among parts of a building.
Eustyle	"**YOU**" "style"	In architecture, the distance between each column is equal to two and a quarter times the diameter of one column.
Ewer	"**YOU**"er	A form of vessel with a wide spout and handle.
Exergue	ig **ZURG** **EK** surg	The small space below the device on a coin or medal.

F

Fabergé, Carl	fa bur **ZHAY** fa "bear" **ZHAY**	A Russian goldsmith and jeweler (1846-1920).
Faenza	fah **EN** zuh	A leading pottery center in Italy famous for its majolica during the 15ᵗʰ to late 16ᵗʰ century.
Faïence	fay **AHNS** fie fa **YAH(N)S**	The French name for tin-glazed earthenware, derived from the Italian town of Faenza.
Faïence Fine	...**FEEN**	The French name used to describe cream-colored earthenware or lead-glazed white pottery.
Faïence Japonnée	...zha pun **NAY**	The 18ᵗʰ century French name for faïence decorated with enamel in an oriental manner.
Faïence Parlante	...par **LAH(N)T**	The French name for faïence wares having inscriptions in their decorative motifs.
Faïence Patriotique	...pa tree yuh **TEEK**	The French name for faïence decorated with patriotic motifs.
Faille	fa^{yuh}	(Fr.) A woven cloth having a corded effect.
Falchion or Fauchon	"**FALL**" chun **FOL** chun	A type of sword used during the Middle Ages.
Faldstool	"**FALL**"(**D**) stool	A portable folding stool.

Famille	fuh mee	(Fr.) Family
Famille Jaune	...**ZHONE**	A Chinese porcelain characterized by a dominant yellow ground.
Famille Noire	...**NWAHR**	A Chinese porcelain characterized by a dominant black ground.
Famille Rose	...**"ROSE"**	A Chinese porcelain characterized by a dominant pink or crimson ground.
Famille Verte	...**VAIRT**	A Chinese porcelain characterized by shades of green predominating.
Fang Lei	fahng lay	(Ch.) A tall, rectangular vase with cover.
Fasces	**FA** "seize"	A bundle of rods containing an ax in the middle.
Fascia	**FAY** shah **FA** shah	In architecture, a flat, horizontal member.
Faubourg	**FOE** bourg foe **BOOR**	
Faubourg St. Antoine	...sa(n)t ah(n) **TWAHN**	(Fr.) A tapestry manufactory founded in the Faubourg St. Antoine in 1597.
Faubourg Saint-Denis or Faubourg Saint-Lazare	...sa(n) duh **NEE** ...sa(n) lah **ZAHR**	(Fr.) A hard paste porcelain factory founded in Paris in 1771.
Faubourg St. Germain	...sa(n) zhair **MA(N)**	(Fr.) A tapestry manufactory founded in Paris in the Faubourg St. Germain in the early 17th century

Faubourg Saint-Lazare	...sa(n) lah **ZAHR**	See *Faubourg Saint-Denis*
Faubourg St. Marceau	...sa(n) mahr "**SO**"	See *Gobelins*
Fauchard	foe shahr	A pole arm used during the 16th century
Fauldesteuil or Faudesteuil	foe duh "**STIR**" foe duh "**STIR**"^{yuh}	(Fr.) A medieval type of chair characterized by its curving X-shaped legs.
Fauteuil	foe tur foh **TU(R)**^{yuh}	(Fr.) An armchair.
Fauteuil Canné	..."can" **NAY**	(Fr.) A caned armchair.
Fauteuil de Bureau	...duh byou **ROE**	(Fr.) A desk or writing chair.
Fauteuil de Bureau à Tournant	...ah "tour" **NAH(N)**	(Fr.) A desk chair with a swivel seat.
Fauves, Les	fohv lay	(Fr. 'wild beasts') A group of early 20th century French artists who collectively led the first major aesthetic movement.
Favrile	fuhv **REEL**	Iridescent art glass wares invented and produced by Louis C. Tiffany.
Fei-Ts'ui Jade	fay-dzue ay	(Ch.) A type of emerald green jade.
Felletin Tapestries	fell **TA(N)**	(Fr.) A 16th century tapestry center in the village of Felletin.
Fêng-Huang	fung-whahng	A Chinese decorative art motif of an imaginary phoenix-like bird.
Feng Shui	fung **SHWAY**	(Ch.) A philosophy placing people and objects in harmony with their surroundings.

F

Feretory	"**FAIR**" uh tory	A shrine in which the remains or relics of saints were kept.
Ferrara Tapestries	fuh **RAH** ruh feh **RAH** rah	(It.) A 16th century tapestry factory founded at Ferrara.
Ferronnerie	"fair" run **REE**	(Fr.) A type of wrought-iron work.
Fête Champêtre	fet shah(m) **PET**ruh	(Fr. 'outdoor feast') A type of Rococo genre painting.
Fête Galante	fet ga **LAH(N)T**	(Fr. 'feast of courtship') A type of Rococo genre painting.
Feuille de Chou	fu(r)yuh duh "shoe"	(Fr. 'cabbage leaf') A decoration characterized by overlapping raised leaves, used on Chinese armorial and export porcelain.
Feuilles d'Acanthe	fu(r)yuh da **KAH(N)T**	(Fr.) Acanthus leaves.
Figa	**FEE** gah	(Braz.) The fingers of a hand positioned in a way to ward off the evil eye.
Filet	fee **LAY**	
Filet Brodé à Reprisés	...bro **DAY** ah ruh pree **ZAY**	(Fr.) A form of netted or darned lace.
Filet Guipure	...ghee "pure"	(Fr.) A form of netted or darned lace.
Filigree	"**FILL**" i gree	In jewelry, a delicate, ornamental work of fine wire, usually gold or silver.
Fillet	"**FILL**" it	In architecture, a narrow, flat molding.
Fin-de-siècle	fa(n)-duh-**SYEK**luh	(Fr.) End of the 19th century.
Fior di Persica	fyor dee "**PAIR**" see kah	(It.) A type of violet-colored marble from Seravezza, Tuscany.

Flabellum	fluh **BELL** um	A fan used in religious ceremonies during the early Christian era.
Flagellum	fluh "**JELL**" um	A whip.
Flambé	flahm **BAY** flah(m) **BAY**	A Chinese glaze of rich red color marbled with grey and purple.
Flambeau	**FLAM** boe flah(m) **BOE**	A candlestick or torch.
Flanchard	**FLANK** urd	A medieval plate of armor for a horse's flank.
Flâneuse	fla **NU(R)Z**	(Fr.) A type of lounge chair.
Fleur-de-Lis or Fleur-de-Lys	flur-duh-**LEE** flur-duh-**LEEZ**	(Fr.) A term for the iris flower. Also, a heraldic ornamental device representing the lily.
Fleur de Pêcher	flur duh peh **SHAY**	A type of violet-colored marble from Seravezza, Tuscany.
Fleuri Marble	flur **REE**	A type of dark-colored marble from Carcassonne, Aude, France.
Fleur Volante	flur voh **LAH(N)T**	(Fr.) A lace-making term meaning flying flower.
Fleurs Chatironnées	flur sha tee "run" **NAY**	(Fr.) A term to describe a style of flower painting using enamel colors.
Fleurs des Indes	flur day **ZA(N)D**	(Fr.) A term used for the floral motifs derived from oriental ceramics.
Flintporslin	flint pors "**LEAN**"	A Swedish term for a cream-colored earthenware in the English style.
Florentine	"**FLOOR**" un teen "**FLOOR**" un tine	Pertaining to Florence, Italy.

F

Fond	"fond" foh(n)	(Fr.) A lace-making term meaning background or groundwork.
Fond Chant	...shah(n)	(Fr.) A lace-making term for a six-pointed star riseau or ground.
Fond de Neige	...duh **NEZH**	(Fr.) A lace-making term for ground having a snow-like appearance.
Fond Écaille	...ay **KAH**^{yuh}	(Fr.) In ceramics, a high-temperature glaze the color of tortoiseshell.
Fondi d'Oro	**FON** dee **DOE** roe	(It.) A method of using gold foil on glass as a decorative element.
Fond Simple	...**SA(M)** pl^{uh}	(Fr.) A lace-making term for the thinnest, most transparent lace ground.
Fontainebleau	foh(n) ten "**BLOW**"	(Fr.) A 16th century Royal Tapestry Factory Manufactory set up by François I at Fontainebleau.
Foyer	**FOY** ur **FOY** yay	A lobby or entrance hall.
Fractur or Fraktur	"frock" "**TOUR**"	An illuminated style of decorative writing used by the Pennsylvania Dutch.
Frailero	"fry" **LEH** roe	(Sp.) A type of monk's chair used during the Spanish Renaissance.
Framea	**FRAY** "me" uh	An ancient German lance.
Franche-Compté	frah(n)sh-coh(m) **TAY**	(Fr.) A provincial style of furniture named for a former province.
François I	frah(n) **SWAH** pruh **MYAY**	A French Renaissance style of ornament after François I, King of France.

Frankenthal	"**FRANK**" in **THALL** **FRAHNK** in "**TALL**"	*(Ger.) A famous 18th century porcelain factory at Frankenthal.*
Frechen	**FREH** shen	*(Ger.) A late 16th century Rhenish stoneware center at Frechen, near Cologne.*
Freiburg	"**FRY**" burg	*(Ger.) A late 17th century pottery center known for its grey stoneware jugs.*
Frêne Wood	frehn	*A hard, white and yellowish-brown striped wood of the ash tree.*
Fresco	**FRES** koe	*A type of mural painting using permanent limestone pigments on a fresh lime plaster.*
Fresquera	fres **KEH** rah	*(Sp.) A type of ventilated cupboard used for storing food.*
Friesian	**FREE** zhun **FREE** zhee un	*A Pennsylvania Dutch wheel-form scratch carving technique, used on boxes, chests, etc.*
Friesland	frees lahnd	*(Dut.) A faïence center located at Friesland until the 19th century.*
Frieze	"freeze"	*A horizontal band usually decorated with relief sculpture.*
Frottage	fraw **TAHZH** fruh	*(Fr.) A technique of reproducing a texture by means of rubbing lead or chalk, etc. over paper laid on the object.*
Frottis	fruh **TEE**	*(Fr.) A thin wash of paint.*
Fu	foo	*A Chinese symbol for a bat used as a decorative motif. Also, a type of Bronze Age food vessel.*

F

Fuchi	foo chee	*(Jap.) An ornamental ring around the hilt of the sword or dagger next to the guard.*
Fu-hsing	foo-sheeng	*(Ch.) A popular Taoist deity.*
Fujiwara	foo jee wah lah	*(Jap.) A late Heian period (897-1185).*
Fukien	foo k^{ee}en	*(Ch.) A famous ceramic province.*
Fulda	**FOOL** ah	*(Ger.) An 18th century faïence factory founded at Fulda, Hesse.*
Fumage	fue **MAHZH**	*(Fr.) A collage using smoked paper as well as other materials.*
Fumeuse	fue **MU(R)Z**	*(Fr.) A type of 18th century chair similar to the chaise à accoudoir.*
Fundame	foon dah meh	*A form of Japanese lacquer process.*
Furstenberg	**"FIRST"** en **BAIRK**	*(Ger.) A porcelain factory founded in 1747 at Brunswick.*
Fusain Wood	**"FEW"** zane	*A hard, pale yellow wood of the spindle tree.*
Fu Shou An Ling	foo "show" ahn leeng	*Chinese characters signifying happiness, long life, peace and spirit.*
Fustian	**"FUSS"** chun	*A coarse fabric of cotton and flax.*
Fylfot	**"FILL"** faht	*A painted device to fill the lower part of a colored window. Also, an early name for the swastika.*

G

| Gadroon | guh **DROON** | *A decorative border of repeated lobed ornaments of straight or curved shape.* |

| Gaichi | **"GAY"** chee | *In rug weaving, a type of scissors used to trim yarn ends.* |

| Gaine | ghen | *(Fr.) A pedestal.* |

| Gallé, Émile | ga **LAY**, ay **"MEAL"** | *French glassmaker and furniture designer (1846-1904).* |

| Gallipot | **GAL** uh "pot" | *A small porcelain container used by apothecaries and painters.* |

| Gama Ishime | gah mah ee shee meh | *(Jap.) A form of decoration on the metal of the background of Japanese sword mounts. Resembles the skin of a toad.* |

| Garde-de-bras | "guard"-duh-**BRAH** | *(Fr.) In armor, 15th century plate armor for the arm.* |

| Garde-de-reine | "guard"-duh-**REN** | *(Fr.) In armor, a guard of plate to protect the loins.* |

| Garde du Vin | "guard" due **VA(N)** | *(Fr.) A wine cooler.* |

| Garde-Manger | "guard"-mah(n) **ZHAY** | *(Fr.) A cupboard with pierced doors used to store food.* |

| Garderobe | **GAHR** drobe
gahr duh **"RUB"** | *(Fr.) A wardrobe or armoir for clothes.* |

| Garfagnana, rosso | gahr fah **NYAH** nah, **ROH** soh | *Italian marble having a pink and white ground and reddish-brown veins.* |

Garniture de Cheminée	gahr nee ture duh shuh mee **NAY**	(Fr.) A set of ornaments used on the mantlepiece.
Gascogne	"gas" **CUN**^{yuh}	An old province in southwestern France and a main source for Louis XIII-style provincial furniture.
Gaudi, Antonio y Cornet	**GOW** dee gow **DEE** ahn **TOE** nee oh ee "core" **NET**	Catalonian architect and designer (1856-1926).
Gaufrage	goh **FRAHZH**	(Fr.) A technique employed in textiles to produce relief ornament by pressure.
Geburtsschein	geh **BOORTS** shine	(Ger.) A birth certificate.
Gemel Bottle	**JEM** ul	A bottle consisting of two flasks fused together with the necks going in opposite directions.
Genouillière	zhuh noo **YAIR**	In armor, a medieval protective covering for the knee.
Genre	zhahn^{ruh} zhah(n)^{ruh}	Un-idealized paintings that portray scenes from everyday life.
Gentese	jen "**TEASE**"	In architecture, a term for cusps found in the arch of a doorway.
Gera	**GEH** rah	(Ger.) A faïence factory started at Gera, Thuringia in 1752. The porcelain factory was founded there in 1779.
Gesamtkunstwerk	guh zahmt koonst vairk	(Ger.) The concept of a complete integration of all art forms.
Gesso	**JEH** "so"	A white primer used both as a ground for painting canvas, wood, and other decorative processes.

Ghashoghdoun	**GAHS OHG** "dune"	A small storage bag.
Ghiordes	**GYOR** dus **GOR** dus	A Turkish knot used in rug weaving. Also, an oriental rug of Turkish origin, best known as prayer rugs.
Gien	zh^{ee}e(n)	(Fr.) A pottery factory founded here in 1864.
Giglio	**JEE** lee oh	(It.) An ornamental element resembling the fleur-de-lis.
Girandole or Gerondole	"**JEER**" un dole	A branched candelabrum; an ornate wallbracket for candelabra. In jewelry, a brooch or earring.
Girouette	zhee roo **ET**	(Fr.) A type of weathervane.
Gisant	zhee zah(n)	(Fr.) A tomb with sculptured representation of the deceased in a recumbent position.
Gisarme or Guisarme	zhee **ZAHRM** ghee	A medieval shafted weapon.
Giustiniani	"juice" teen **YAH** nee	(It.) A porcelain and pottery factory established in Naples during the latter part of the 18th century.
Glace	"glass"	(Fr.) A mirror.
Glaive	glave	A medieval sword or broadsword.
Gobelins	**GO** buh lins guh **BLA(N)**	The tapestry factory in Paris named after its founders. It was made a royal manufactory in 1662.
Gobelin Stitch	**GO** buh lin **GAH**	A tapestry stitch; an upright stitch.

G

Godendag	**HOE** dun dah[gh]	A medieval Flemish weapon having a spiked end.
Godet	go **DET**	A late medieval shallow-handled cup.
Goffer or Gauffer	**GAHF** ur	An ornamental frill, ruffle, etc. Also, a surface decorated by embossing or indenting it.
Göggingen	**GUR** ging[in]	(Ger.) A faïence factory established near Angsburg, Bavaria in 1748.
Gomoku-Zōgan	goh moh koo-zoh gahn	(Jap.) A type of metal decoration found on tsuba and other sword fittings.
Gonçalo Alves Wood	gun **SA** "low" **AL** vis	A hard, close-textured wood from Brazil; straw-colored with dark streaks.
Gondole, En	goh(n) "**DULL**", ah(n)	(Fr.) A term referring to inwardly curving arms of seat-furniture between 1740-1770.
Gonome Nanako	goh noh meh nah nah koh	(Jap.) A type of nanako (surface decoration) found on sword mounts.
Göppingen	**GUR** ping[in]	(Ger.) A faïence factory established at Göppingen, Württemberg in 1741.
Gorevan Rug	**GOR** uh vahn	An oriental rug of Persian origin.
Gorge-de-Pigeon	gorzh-duh-pee **ZHOH(N)**	(Fr.) A form of opaline glass.
Gorgerin	**GAW** juh rin	In architecture, the part of the column just below the top molding, or between the shaft and the capital.
Gorget	**GOR** jit	In armor, a protective steel collar for the throat.

Gorgoneion	gor "**GO**" nee un	An ornament representing the head of a gorgon; e.g., Medusa.
Gotha	**GOH** tah	(Ger.) A porcelain factory founded at Gotha, Thuringia, in 1757.
Gouache	gwahsh goo **AHSH**	(Fr.) An opaque watercolor.
Gozame Ishime	goh zah meh ee shee meh	(Jap.) A type of surface decoration on sword mounts resembling a straw mat.
Graffiato	grah fee **AH** toh	see Sgraffiato
Graffito	gruh **FEE** doe grahf **FEE** toh *pl.* -tee	(It.) A drawing or writing scratched on walls.
Grand Feu	grah(n) fu(r)	(Fr.) A term for a high-temperature kiln (1200-1400 degrees Celsius).
Grapen	grahp^{un}	(Ger.) A ceramic cooking vessel of tripod form.
Gravure	gruh **V"YOUR"**	An intaglio printing process, such as photogravure or rotogravure.
Greave	"grieve"	In armor, plate armor for the legs, between the knee and the ankle. Also called a jamb or jambeau.
Grès	greh	(Fr.) A term for stoneware.
Grès de Flandres	greh duh **FLAH(N)** dr^{uh}	An old name for salt-glazed stoneware.
Greuby Faïence Co.	"**GREW**" bee fay **AHNS**	An American art pottery company founded at Boston in 1897.

G

Griotte	gree **YUT**	A marble found in the Pyrenees that is dark green, or red and purple.
Grisaille	griz "**ALE**" gree **ZAH**yuh	(Fr.) A monochrome painting done in grays.
Gros Bleu	"grow" **BLU(R)**	In porcelain, a dark blue underglaze color introduced at Sèvres and Vincennes around 1749-1760.
Gros de Tours	"grow" duh **TOOR**	(Fr.) A type of corded cloth used for covering seat-furniture in the late 17th and 18th century.
Gros Point	"grow" **PWA(N)**	A large embroidery stitch on a canvas or mesh ground.
Gros Point de Venise	"grow" pwa(n) duh vuh **NEEZ**	See Punto Tagliato a Fogliami
Groszbreitengach	"Gross" "Brighton" "Bach"	(Ger.) A porcelain factory, still in existence, founded at Groszbreitenbach, Thuringia around 1778.
Grünstadt	groon shtaht	(Ger.) A factory founded at Grünstadt in 1801, known for making cream-colored earthenware.
Gryphon	"griffin"	An American heraldic beast, half eagle and half lion.
Guadamací	gwah thah mah **SEE**	(Sp.) A term for finely tooled leather with elaborately painted and gilded designs.
Guaiac Wood	G"**WHY**" ack	A very hard green and black striped wood also called holy wood from French Guiana.

Guarea Wood	**GWAH** ree uh	A pinkish-colored wood from West Africa. Often referred to as pink mahogany or African cedar.
Gubbio	**GOO** byoh	(It.) A majolica center at Gubbio from the 15ᵗʰ century.
Guendje Rug or Genghis	ghen jeh	An oriental rug of Caucasian origin.
Guéridon	"gay" ree **DOH(N)**	(Fr.) A small stand or table suitable for supporting a candelabrum.
Guérite	"gay" **REET**	(Fr.) A type of hooded chair.
Gueuse	gu(r)z	The feminine form of a French word meaning 'beggar', referring to an inferior quality of bobbin lace.
Guglet	**GUG** lit	A long-necked container, usually earthenware.
Guijo Wood	**GHEE** hoe **GWEE** hoe	A hard reddish wood from the Philippines.
Guilloche	gi "**LOW**"SH ghee **YUSH**	(Fr.) A running ornament formed of interlaced curved lines.
Guimpe	gamp gimp	Yolk of lace or embroidery, etc.
Guipure	ghee **PURE**	(Fr.) Any of various laces where the design units were supported by brides rather than by a net ground.
Gul	"ghoul"	'Flower'; an octagonal decorative motif found on oriental rugs. Also called elephant's footprint.

G

Guli Hinnai Motif
  or
Gul-henna
	gohl ha na[ee]
	
	"ghoul"-hen **AY**
		(Per.) 'Henna blossom'; a design
		  motif used on Persian rugs.

Gulestan or Gulistan	**GOO** lis tan	An oriental rug of Persian origin.
Guri	goo lee	(Jap.) A type of lacquer work.
Guri Bori	goo lee boh lee	(Jap.) A decorative work on sword mounts in imitation of Guri lacquer.
Guttae	"**GUT**" ee	In architecture, the small drop ornaments below the regula in the mutules of the Doric order. Also, in mid-18th century furniture, feet in the form of guttae used on chair and table legs.

H

Haarlem	hahr lem	(Dut.) A pottery center established here in the 16th century.
Hachure	ha **SHOOR** **HASH** oor	Hatching, short parallel lines. In cartography, short, thin parallel lines.
Hafner Ware	**HAHF** ner	(Ger. 'stove-maker') Tiles and vessels made by the stone-makers of Germany, Austria and Switzerland from the middle of the 14th century onwards.
Hagi-Yaki	hah ghee-yah kee	(Jap.) A pottery made near Hagi, as early as the 16th century
Haguenau	ahg **NOH**	(Fr.) A branch of the Hannong porcelain and pottery factory, established in Haguenau, Alsace, in 1723.
Hallenkirche	**HAH** len **KEER** huh	A term referring to a church whose aisles and nave are of equal height.
Hamadan Rug	**HAM** uh dan **HAHM** uh dahn	An oriental rug of Persian origin.
Hanau Pottery	**HAH** now	(Ger.) A faïence factory established at Hanau, near Frankfurt-am-Main in 1661.
Haniwa	hah nee wah	(Jap.) In ceramics, a term for unglazed red clay figures.
Hansje in den Kelder	**HANS** yur in dan **KAL** dur	(Dut.) A 17th century drinking vessel, usually of silver.

Haricot	**HAR** uh koe **HAR** uh "cot" ah ree **KOH**	(Fr. 'bean') A crescent-shaped small table.
Hari Ishime	hah lee ee shee meh	(Jap.) A surface decoration of small openings on sword fittings as if pricked by a needle.
Harlingen	hahr lin(g) un	(Dut.) A faïence factory established in 1598 at Harlingen in Friesland.
Harquebus	"R" kuh "bus" **HAHR** kwuh "bus"	Any of several small-caliber matchlock or wheel-lock guns dating from around the 1400's.
Hasami	hah sah mee	(Jap.) An important pottery center for Japanese-style tea utensils.
Hatchlou or Hatchlu, Hatchli	"**HATCH**" loo	(Arm.) A large design used on carpets and tent door-hangings.
Hauberk	**HAW** burk	A medieval long coat-of-mail.
Häufebecher	**HOY** fuh **BEH** "care"	(Ger.) A late 16th-early 17th century small cup made to be fitted into another one.
Hausmalerei	"**HOUSE**" mah luh "**RYE**"	(Ger.) Free-lance faïence and porcelain painters of the late 17th to 18th century.
Haute-Lisse	"oat"-"lease"	(Fr.) A high-warp tapestry.
Haut-Relief	oh-"relief" oh-ruh **LYEF**	(Fr.) High relief.
Heaume	"home"	In armor, a 13th century headpiece.
Hehbehlik	hay bay "**LICK**"	A Perso-Turkish word used to describe a saddle bag.

Heian	heh ee ahn	A Japanese time period. Jogan (Early Heian) 794-897; Fujiwara (Late Heian) 897-1185.
Helladic	heh **LAD** ik	Pertaining to the Bronze Age culture on the Greek mainland (c 2900-1100 B.C.).
Hellenic Art	heh **LEN** ik	Pertaining to the art and culture of the ancient Greeks (1100-100 B.C.)
Hematite	"**HE**" muh tite	A stone sometimes used for decorative inlays and carvings.
Henri Deux Ware	ah(n) ree du(r)	(Fr.) See Saint-Porchaire
Herat	heh **RAHT**	A classification of Persian carpets.
Herati Motif	heh "**ROD**" ee	A common repeating design found in Persian rugs.
Hereke	heh ree **KAY**	A Turkish oriental rug woven at Herek-Keui.
Herend	**HEH** rend	A Hungarian porcelain factory founded at Herend in 1838.
Herez Rug or Heriz	huh **REZ** heh **REEZ**	An oriental rug of Persian origin. Also, an established weaving district.
Hermaphrodite	her **MAF** ruh dite	An artistic motif; a figure in which male and female reproductive organs are combined.
Herrebøe	"hair" bu(r)	An important Norwegian porcelain factory founded near Friedrichshald in 1757.
Hêtre Wood	**ET**ruh	A semi-hard white wood of the beech tree.

H

Hibachi	hi **BAH** chee	A charcoal brazier covered with a grill.
Hidasuki	hee dah soo kee	(Jap. 'cross-fire') In ceramics, a decorating technique.
Hieracosphinx	"**HIGHER**" **AY** koe sfinx	A sculptured hawk-headed lion.
Hieroglyphics	"**HIGH**" roe gli "fix"	A picture or symbol representing a sound, word, or syllable.
Hirado Ware	hi **RAH** doe	(Jap.) A type of blue and white porcelain made at Mikawachi near Arita from the mid-17th century.
Hirame	hee lah meh	(Jap.) A type of lacquer decoration using gold or silver leaf.
Hirasa or Hirase	hee lah sah hee lah seh	(Jap.) In ceramics, a kiln located at Hirasa.
Hira-Zōgan	hee lah-zoh gahn	(Jap.) In sword mounts, a flat inlay.
Hispano-Moresque	hi **SPA** "no"-muh **RESK** ee **SPAH** noh-muh **RESK**	A lustre pottery made in Spain by Moorish potters from the 13th -15th century.
Hizen Ware	**HEE** zen	(Jap.) An important province known for its ceramics.
Ho Chou	huh choe	(Chi.) In ceramics, a pottery located at Ho Chou, as early as the T'ang dynasty.
Hochschnitt	"hawk" shnit	(Ger.) An engraving technique on glass where decoration appears in relief.
Höchst	hurkst hekst	(Ger.) A pottery and porcelain factory founded near Mayence in 1746.

Höhr	"her"	An important 16th century German center for salt-glazed stoneware.
Holitsch	"**HOE**" "leach"	A Hungarian faïence factory started in 1743 at Holitsch.
Honan Celadon	huh nahn **SELL** uh dahn	(Chi.) In ceramics, celadon kilns in the northern province of Honan.
Honan Temmoku	huh nahn tem moh koo	(Chi.) In ceramics, a name applied to a variety of Chinese Sung black and tan glazed wares made in the province of Honan.
Honiton	**HAHN** eh "ton"	An early English lace made around 1620-1725.
Hon-Zōgan	hohn-zoh gahn	(Jap.) A decorative inlay process using gold or silver wire.
Hôpital de la Trinité	oh pee **TAHL** duh lah tree nee **TAY**	(Fr.) A tapestry factory established at the Hôpital de la Trinité in Paris by King Henri II in the mid-16th century.
Horologium	hoe roe **LOE** jee um	A timepiece.
Hotei	hoh teh ee	(Jap.) One of the seven household gods.
Houx Wood	oo	(Fr.) A fine grained, almost white wood of the holly tree.
Hsiang	sh^{ee}ahng	(Chi.) An elephant figure.
Hsien	sh^{ee}en	(Chi.) A two-part vessel for domestic and ritual use.
Hsien Fêng	sh^{ee}en fung	(Chi.) A reign of the Ch'ing dynasty (1851-1861).

H

Hsi Wang Mu	shee wahng moo	(Chi.) A Taoist goddess of long life.
Hsüan-Chi	sh^{ue}en-chee	(Chi.) A type of ritual jade.
Hsüan-Tê	sh^{ue}en-tuh	A reign of the Ming dynasty (1426-1435).
Hsüan T'ung	sh^{ue}en tohng	(Chi.) A reign of the Ch'ing dynasty (1909-1912).
Hu	"who"	(Chi.) A Bronze Age jug-shaped wine storage vessel. In art, a tiger figure.
Huche	oosh	(Fr.) A kneading trough, hutch, or type of bin.
Huche à pain	oosh ah pa(n)	(Fr.) A bread chest.
Huguenot Silver	"**HUGH**" guh "not" oog **NOH**	A silver made by or in the style of the Huguenot refugees.
Humpen	**HOOM** pen	(Ger.) A large, cylindrical type of drinking vessel.
Hung Chih	hohng j^{uh}	(Chi.) A reign of the Ming dynasty (1488-1505).
Hung Hsi	hohng shee	(Chi.) A reign of the Ming dynasty (1425).
Hung Wu	hohng oo	(Chi.) A reign of the Ming dynasty (1368-1398).
Hu P'i	"who" pee	(Chi.) A type of ceramic ware that combines different colored glazes.
Hypaethral	"hi" **PEE** thral	(Gk.) A term descriptive of an ancient Greek roofless temple.
Hypogeum	"hi" puh **GEE** um	The underground part of a building.

I

Ichnography	ik **NAH** gruh fee	A scale drawing of the ground plan of a building.
Iconostasis	"i" kuh **NAHS** tuh sis	In the Eastern Christian Church, a partition or screen on which icons are placed, separating the sanctuary from the main body of the church.
Iga	ee gah	(Jap.) In ceramics, a pottery center in Iga as early as the mid-5th century.
Igel	"eagle"	(Ger.) A 16th century type of green glass vessel covered with prunts or glass studs.
Ikat	**EE** kaht	An Indonesian term to describe a method of printing woven fabric by tie-dyeing.
Ilmenau	"ill" muh now	(Ger.) A porcelain factory founded at Ilmenau, Thuringia in 1777.
Imagiers	ee ma **ZHYAY**	(Fr.) Sculptors and stone carvers supervised by the clergy who carved and decorated Gothic churches and cathedrals.
Imari	uh **MAHR** ee	A richly decorated Japanese porcelain made at Arita for the export trade.
Imbe	eem beh	(Jap.) In ceramics, a type of stoneware made for the tea ceremony, first produced in the province Bizen in the 16th century.

Impasto	em **PAHS** toh	*(It.) A thick application of pigment.*
Incuse	in "**CUES**" in **KYOOS**	*Hammered or stamped in, i.e., a design or figure on a coin.*
Indianische Blumen	in di **AH** ni shuh " **BLOOMIN'** "	*(Ger.) In ceramics, a term used for the floral motifs derived from oriental porcelain.*
Indiennes	a(n) dee **EN**	*(Fr.) A term referring to the chintz and calicoes brought into Europe from India.*
Inely	**IN** lee	*(Anat. 'good') A term used for the best rugs from Moden.*
Intaglio	in **TAL** yoh in **TAG** lee oh een **TAH** lyoh	*(It.) An incised hollow-cut design.*
Intaglio-Rilievato	... ree lyeh **VAH** toe	*(It.) A type of intaglio practiced by the early Egyptians.*
Intarsia	in "**TAR**" see uh	*(It.) Inlay work; a type of marquetry.*
Intonaco	in toh "**KNOCK**" oh	*(It.) In fresco painting, the final layer of plaster.*
Ionic	"eye" **AH** nik	*The Greek order of architecture characterized by the spiral volutes of its capital.*
Ipek	**IH** pek	*(Tur.) The word for silk.*
Iserlohn	**EE** z^{er} lohn	*(Ger.) Mid-18th century metal boxes used for snuff or tobacco with embossed or engraved lids, made at Iserlohn in Westphalia.*
Ishime	ee shee meh	*(Jap.) The background of sword fittings. Also, a surface resembling the texture of stone.*

Ishi-zuri	ee shee-zoo lee	(Jap.) Stone-print.
Isfahan or Ispahan	**ISS** fuh hahn	A Persian city under the Safavid dynasty; currently a fine rug-making center.
Isocephalic	"eye" "so" suh **FAL** ik	In fine arts, the practice of modifying natural proportions so that all figures are approximately on the same level.
Istoriato	ee stoh ree **AH** toh	(It.) A late 15th and 16th century majolica decorated with all-over pictorial scenes.
Ito Sukashi	ee toh soo kah shee	(Jap.) A form of decorative work found on the tsuba.
Iwakura Ware	ee wah koo lah	(Jap.) A 17th century pottery made near Kyoto.
Izumo Ware	ee tzoo moh	(Jap.) A pottery made at Izumo during the mid-18th century.

J

Jabot	zha **BOE**	*A frill, usually of lace, attached to the neck of a blouse or shirt.*
Jacinth	**JAY** sinth	*In jewelry, a variety of zircon.*
Jacobean	"**JACK**" o "**BEE**" un	*A style of architecture, furniture, and decoration employed in England during the reign of James I (1603-25).*
Jacquard	ja "**CARD**" "**JACK**" ahrd	*A patterned fabric produced on a Jacquard loom. Also, a type of hand loom for producing complicated patterns.*
Jadeite	**JAY** dite	*True jade, whitish to dark green in color.*
Jakobakrug or Jakobakanne	yah koh bah kroog yah koh bah kahn^uh	*(Ger.) A tall, slender ceramic jug with a ring handle.*
Jalousie	**JA** luh see	*A type of window blind or shutter.*
Jamb	jam	*A vertical side of a window, door, or other opening.*
Jambeau	**JAM** boe	*In armor, see Greave.*
Jambiya	jam **BEE** yuh	*An Arabian knife.*
Japonaiserie	jap uh nuz uh **REE** jap uh **NEZ** uh ree zha poh neh **ZREE**	*(Fr.) European imitations of Japanese works of art.*

Japonisme	zha poh "**KNEES**" ^{muh}	(Fr.) The Japanese influence on European art.
Jardinière	jahrd'n **EAR** zhar dee **NYAIR**	(Fr.) An ornamental stand for flower pots.
Jarretière	zhar **TYAIR**	(Fr.) A type of bracelet usually of metal with a buckle on one end.
Jaune Jonquille	zhohn zhoh(n) **KEE**	(Fr.) A yellow ground color found on Sèvres porcelain around 1752.
Jever	yay vuh	(Ger.) A faïence factory established at Oldenburg in 1760.
Jimigaki	jee mee gah kee	(Jap.) The polished surfaces on metal work.
Joaillerie	zhuh a^{yuh} **REE**	(Fr.) Jewelry composed mainly of gemstones.
Jogan	"joe" gahn	A Japanese time period (794-897).
Joshaghan or Djushaghan	joh sheh gahn	An oriental rug of Persian origin. Also, a rug-producing village north of Isfahan.
Jours	zhoor	Decorative stitches used to fill in the enclosed spaces in lacemaking.
Ju Ware	roo	(Chi.) A fine stoneware made at Ju Chou in central Honan for imperial use in the early 12th century.
Juan Ts'ai	rahn tsie	(Chi.) In ceramics, a name given to soft enamels.
Ju-i	roo^{ee}	(Chi.) A conventionalized motif found in ceramics.
Jugendstil	you gunt shteel	(Ger. 'young style') The Austrian and German term for Art Nouveau.

J

| Jukushi | joo koo shee | *(Jap. 'ripe persimmon') In ceramics, a term given to a Raku tea bowl made by Donyu.* |
| Jungfrauenbecher | **YOONK FROW**'n **BECK** ehr | *(Ger.) A late 16th and 17th century drinking vessel in the form of a girl.* |

K

Kaba	**KA** bah	In oriental rugs, a prefix frequently heard at auctions meaning 'coarse'.
Kaba-Karaman	**KAH** bah -kah rah **MAHN**	An oriental rug of Turkish origin.
Kabistan or Cabistan	"**CAB**" is tan **KAHB** is tahn	An oriental rug of Caucasian origin.
Kabuto Gane	kah boo toh gah neh	(Jap.) The pommel of a tachi, a state sword.
Kabuzuchi	kah boo tzoo chee	(Jap.) A knob or pommel.
Kachina Doll	kuh **CHEE** nuh	A carved, wooden Hopi Indian doll in representation of a supernatural being.
Kago-Ami	kah goh-ah mee	(Jap.) An ornamental diaper pattern resembling woven bamboo.
Kaiba	**KIE** bah kah ah bah	A Caucasian term for a specific rug size.
Kairaku-en Ware	kah ee lah koo-en	(Jap.) The made-to-order porcelain for the feudal chief of the province of Kishu.
Kaiserteller	"kaiser" "teller"	(Ger.) An elaborately made pewter platter.
Kakemono	kah keh moh noh	(Jap.) A vertical hanging scroll.

Kakiemon	kah kee eh mohn	(Jap.) A porcelain decorated with overglaze enamels, named after the famous porcelain maker Sakaida Kakiemon (1596-1666).
Kalathos or Calathus	**KAL** uh thos pl. -thoy	(Gk.) A fruit or wicker basket.
Kaltemail	**KAHL** tuh "mile"	(Ger.) A type of lacquer applied in the 16th and 17th century to imitate enamel.
Kamakura	kah mah koo lah	A Japanese time period (1185-1333).
Kamashimo Zashi	kah mah shee moh zah shee	(Jap.) A type of sword presented to a boy when he first dons his ceremonial dress.
K'ang Hsi	kahng shee	(Chi.) A reign of the Ch'ing dynasty (1662-1722). Also, a porcelain made during that reign.
Kano	kah noh	(Jap.) A school of painting founded in the Chinese tradition during the Muromachi period (1338-1573) by Kano Masonobu.
Kantharos or Cantharus	**KAN** thur us pl. -"rye"	An early Greek two-handled deep bowl.
Kaolin	**KAY** uh lin kay **OH** lin	The whitest and purest clay used in the manufacture of porcelain.
Karabagh	ka ruh **BAH** **KAR** a bar kahr ah **BAHG**	An oriental rug of Caucasian origin.
Kara Dagh	**KAHR** uh **DAH**	An oriental rug of Persian origin.

Kara-Geuz	kah rah-gu(r)z	An oriental rug of Persian origin.
Kara-Kane	kah lah-kah neh	(Jap.) A term for bronze.
Karatsu	kah lah tsoo	(Jap.) A glazed pottery made as early as the 13th century at the town of Karatsu in the Hizen province.
Kas	kahs	(Dut.) A large wardrobe with overhanging cornice.
Kasak	kuh **ZAK** kuh **ZAHK**	See Kazak
Kasane	kah sahn eh	(Jap.) A nest of lacquered trays with lid.
Kasaoka	kah sah oh kah	(Jap.) A pottery center in the Okayama Prefecture.
Kashan or Keshan	kuh **SHAHN**	An oriental rug of Persian origin. Also, a town in central Iran.
Kashgai	"**CASH**" "guy"	Persian nomadic tribes. Also, rugs made by these tribes.
Kashi	**KAH** "she"	Enamelled Islamic tile work produced in Persia and India during the 16th and 17th century.
Kashira	kah shee lah	(Jap.) The cap on the pommel of a knife or sword.
Kashmir	**KAZH** meer	A type of modern oriental rug woven in Kashmir, India.
Katakiri-Bori	kah tah kee lee-boh lee	(Jap.) A decorative technique of incised chiselling on sword fittings.
Katár	**KAH** tahr kuh **TAHR**	The oldest and most characteristic of Indian knives.

K

Katchlie Bokhara or Hatchlie, Khatchli	hash lee boh **KAH** ruh boo **KAH** ruh	An oriental rug of Turkoman origin.
Katemono-ye	kah teh moh noh-yeh	(Jap.) Prints in the form of hanging pictures.
Kayseri or Kaysari, Cesarea	**KIE** za ree	A major rug center and capital of Kayseri province in central Turkey.
Kazak or Kasak, Kazakh	kuh **ZAK** kuh **ZAHK**	An oriental rug of Caucasian origin.
Kebori	keh boh lee	(Jap.) The decorative technique of incised chiselling on metal. Also, a hair-line engraving.
Kelebe	**KEL** uh bee	An ancient mixing bowl characterized by a wide neck and two vertical handles.
Keley or Kelie	"kelly"	A rug size, approximately 8'6" X 5'.
Kellinghusen	**KEL** lin(g) **HOOZ**un	(Ger.) A faïence factory founded at Kellinghusen, Holstein, in the late 18th century.
Kelsterbach	kel stair **BAHK**	(Ger.) A faïence factory founded at Kelsterback (Hesse-Darmstadt) in 1758.
Kenareh or Kenare	ken ah **RAY**	A Persian word to describe wide, long runners.
Keras	**KEH** res	A large drinking horn.
Kermanshah	**CARE** mun shah ker **MAHN** shah	An oriental rug of Persian origin.

Kermes	**KER** miz **KER** meez	(Per.) A natural red pigment obtained from an insect (cochineal) found on the kermes oak.
Kermesse or Kirmess, Kermis	kur **MESS** **KUR** mis	An annual outdoor celebration in the Low Countries (Holland, Belgium, N. France).
Kewblas	**KOO** blahs	(Amer.) Art glass produced in the 1890's by the Union Glass Works at Somerville, MA.
Khasi	**KAH** see	Persian and Indian wall decoration using colored tiles.
Khanjar	**KAN** "jar" **HAN** "jar"	A curved dagger of Muslim countries.
Khiva Bokhara	kee vah boh **KAH** ruh boo **KAH** ruh	Oriental rug of Turkoman origin.
Khorassan or Korassan	"**CORE**" uh sahn **KOH** ras san	Oriental rug of Persian origin.
Khotan	koh tan	Oriental rug of Turkoman origin.
Kiangnan Ting Ware	k^{ee}en nahn teeng	(Chi.) A creamy white glazed ware made during the Ming dynasty.
Kiel	keel	(Ger.) A faïence factory begun at Kiel, Holstein, in 1763.
Kiev	**KEE** "f" **KEE** ev	(Rus.) A faïence factory established at Kiev in 1798.
Kiku-No-Go-Mon	kee koo-noh-goh-mohn	(Jap.) A term for the Imperial chrysanthemum crest.
Kilij	**KUL** lich **KILL** izh	A Turkish sabre.

K

Kilim or Khilim Kelim	kill **LEEM** **KILL** im key **LEEM**	A pileless Middle Eastern rug.
Kimono Tray	keh "**MONA**"	(Jap.) A deep-sided, oblong lacquered tray.
Kindjal	**KIN** jahl	A double-edged knife principally carried by the Cossacks.
Kin-Makie	keen-mah kee eh	(Jap.) In lacquer, a term applied to the gold lacquer.
Kinran-de	keen lahn-deh	(Jap.) A gold brocaded motif used on porcelain.
Kiosk	"**KEY**" ahsk **KIE** ahsk	A small pavilion having one or more sides open.
Kiribame	kee lee bah meh	(Jap.) In metal art, a chiselled design process.
Kiribame-Zōgan	kee lee bah meh-zoh gahn	(Jap.) A decorative technique of inserted inlaying on metal.
Kirigane	kee lee gah neh	(Jap.) A decorative technique using small pieces of gold foil on a surface.
Kirman or Kerman	keer **MAHN** **KER** man	An oriental rug of Persian origin.
Kir-Shehr or Kirshehir	keer-sheh heer ker **SHEER**	An oriental rug of Turkish origin. Also, a major weaving center.
Kiselev	kee see **LOHF**	(Rus.) A porcelain factory near Rechitsy founded in the 1850's by ceramist Afanasii Leont'evich Kiselev.

Kitsch	kich	A term applied to something created of tawdry design and sentiment, appealing to popular taste.
Kiva	**KEE** vah	Pueblo Indian ceremonial chamber.
Kiyomizu Ware	kee yoh mee tzoo	(Jap.) A pottery made in Kiyomizu, a district in Kyoto, during the 17th century.
Klismos	**KLIZ** mahs pl. -moy	An ancient Greek type of chair revived in the late 18th and early 19th century.
Kloster-Veilsdorf	**KLOH** stair-**FILE** storg	(Ger.) A porcelain factory founded in 1760 at Kloster-Veilsdorf, Thuringia.
Knop	nahp	A small round knob or ornament.
Kobako	koh bah koh	(Jap.) An incense box.
Koban	**KOH** bahn	(Jap.) A small, vertical print.
Kochi	koh chee	(Jap.) Type of ceramic ware having colored lead glazes and low relief decoration.
Kodōgu	koh doh goo	(Jap.) A term applied collectively to all of the fittings of a sword or dagger, except the tsuba.
Kogai	koh gah ee	(Jap.) A head pin usually carried in a pocket in the scabbard of a sword or knife.
Kojiri	koh jee lee	(Jap.) The metal tip on a scabbard.
Ko-Katana	koh-kah tah nah	(Jap.) A term often applied to the complete knife carried in the scabbard of the sword.

K

Konieh	**COE** nee uh	An oriental rug of Turkish origin.
Königsberg	ku(r) neeks bairk	(Ger.) A faïence factory founded at Königsberg in 1772.
Kore *pl.* Korai	"**CORE**" ee *pl.* -"eye"	(Gk.) A sculptured form of a female figure during the Archaic period (c. 620-500 B.C.).
Koryo	koh ryo	A Korean historical period (918-1392).
Kornilov	"core" nee lohf	(Rus.) A porcelain factory begun at St. Petersburg in 1835, by Mikhail Kornilov.
Korte Gaardjes	"**COURT**"ᵘʰ **HAHR** cheh	(Dut.) In painting, the 17th century guard room subjects.
Kothon	**KOH** thohn	See Plemochoë
Kouros	**COO** rohs *pl.* -roy	(Gk.) A sculptured form of a young male during the Archaic period (c. 620-500 B.C.).
Kovsh	kohvsh	(Rus.) A boat-shaped vessel of silver or wood used for ladling out drinks.
Ko Yao	guh yow	(Chi.) A type of Chinese stoneware from the latter part of the Southern Sung dynasty (1127-1280).
Kozuka	koh tzoo kah	(Jap.) A small knife found in the sheath in the scabbard of a sword or dagger.
Krautstrunk	krowts trohnk	(Ger.) A green glass tumbler covered with prunts, from the 15th-16th century.

Kreussen	"crow"ee sin	(Ger.) Fine stoneware produced in the late 16th century at Kreussen, near Bayreuth.
Kris	"crease"	See Creese
Ku	goo	A type of Chinese Bronze Age drinking vessel.
Kuan Ware	gwahn	A fine Chinese stoneware of the Southern Sung Period (1127-1280).
Kuan Chün Yao	gwahn jueeen yow	See Chün Yao
Kuang	gwahng	(Chi.) A type of covered vessel used for pouring libations.
Kuang Hsü	gwahng "shoe"	(Chi.) A reign of the Ch'ing dynasty (1875-1908).
Kuan Ti	gwahn dee	(Chi.) A Confucian subject used extensively in the arts. Also, a god of war.
Kuan Yao	gwahn yow	(Chi.) A term applied to all stoneware made for the Imperial Court at the Imperial potteries.
Kuan Yin	gwahn yeen	A Chinese Buddhist goddess.
Kuan Yü	gwahn "you"	(Chi.) A Confucian subject, referred to as Kuan Ti after the 16th century.
Kuchi Beni	koo chee beh nee	(Jap. 'mouth rouge') An iron glazing on the edge of dishes and plates.
Kudinov	koo dee NOHF	(Rus.) A porcelain factory started at Lystsovo, near Moscow, in 1818 by N.S. Kudinov.

K

Kuei	gway	(Chi.) A type of Bronze Age food vessel. Also, a mythical beast having only one foot.
K'uei Hsing	kway sheeng	A Confucian subject used extensively in the arts. Also, the god of literature.
Kuei Kung	gway gohng	(Chi.) In ceramics, extremely delicate open work on later Ming porcelain.
Kukri or Kukery	**KOOK** ree	The principal knife or dagger of the Gurkas of Nepal.
Kulah	koo **LAH**	An oriental rug of Turkish origin. Also, a name of a town.
Kum	ghoom	see Qum
Künersberg	kue nairs bairk	(Ger.) A faïence factory established near Memmingen, Bavaria in 1745.
Kurdistan	**KURD** uh stan **KURD** uh stahn	An oriental rug of Persian origin.
Kurfürstenhumpen	**KOOR** fur sten **HOOM** pin	(Ger.) A late 16th century cylindrical drinking vessel with enamelled decoration of the Emperor of the Holy Roman Empire and the Seven Electors.
Kurikata	koo lee kah tah	(Jap.) A projecting knob on a scabbard to prevent it from slipping through the sash.
Kurk	koork	A word meaning the finest grade of wool.

Kutani Ware	koo tah nee	(Jap.) A porcelain made at Katani in the Kaga province around the middle of the 17th century.
Ku Yüeh Hsüan	goo y^ueh sh^ueen	(Chi.) A type of porcelain produced during the Ch'ing dynasty.
Kuznetsov	kooz nyet **SOHF**	(Rus.) A porcelain factory founded by I. Kuznetsov in 1810 at Novo-Kharitonovo.
Kwacho	kwah choh	(Jap.) A term for a bird-and-flower picture.
Kwaiken	kwah ee ken	(Jap.) An older form of dagger used by women to commit ceremonial suicide.
Kwangtung Yao	gwahng tohng yow	A Chinese province where kilns have been located as early as the T'ang dynasty.
Kwaart	kvahrt	(Dut.) In ceramics, a type of clear lead glaze.
Kyathos	**KIE** uh thahs pl. -thoy	See Cyathus
Kylin	**KEE** lin	A Chinese mythical animal figure.
Kylix	**KIE** lix	See Cylix
Kyo	kee oh	(Jap.) Ceramicware made at Kyoto from the late 18th century onward.
Kyoto	kee **ODO** kee **OTO**	(Jap.) A city in central Japan, well known as a pottery center.

K

L

Labradorite	**LAB** ruh dor ite lab ruh **DOR** ite	A mineral characterized by brilliant metalic tints, often blue and green.
Lac-Burgauté	lak-bur go **TAY**	See Burgauté
Lacca Contrafatta	**LAHK** kah kohn trah **FAH** tah	(It.) An imitation of oriental lacquer.
Lacet	la **SEH**	(Fr.) A braid or cord.
Lacis	la **SEE**	(Fr.) Darned netting or lace.
La Chapelle-des-Pots	lah shah pell-day-**POH**	(Fr.) A pottery center at La Chapelle-des-Pots from the 14ᵗʰ century onward.
La Courtille	lah koor **TEE**ʸᵘʰ	(Fr.) A porcelain factory established near Paris in 1771. Also called Rue Fontaine-au-Roy.
Ladik	lah **DEEK**	An oriental rug of Turkish origin.
Lahore	luh **HORE**	A weaving center in Lahore, India.
Lalique Glass	lah **LEEK**	(Fr.) An art glass created by René Lalique beginning in the early 20ᵗʰ century.
Lalique, René	lah **LEEK**, ruh **NAY**	A Parisian Art Nouveau glassmaker and jeweler (1860-1945).
Lambrequin	**LAM** bur kin **LAH(M)** bruh ka(n)	(Fr.) The scarf used as a covering for a medieval helmet. Also, a drapery hung from a cornice or shelf.

Lamé	la **MAY**	*(Fr.) A woven cloth, usually of gold and/or silver metal threads.*
Lamellé	la muh **LAY**	*In leather work, a type of decorative technique.*
Lamerie, Paul	lam **REE**	*An English silversmith (1688-1751).*
La Moncloa	lah mohn **KLOH** ah	*(Sp.) A porcelain factory founded near Madrid in 1817.*
Lampas	**LAM** pus	*A patterned satin, sometimes ornamented with metallic thread.*
Lanai	lah **NIE** lah **NAH** ee	*An open-sided living room.* *In Hawaii, a veranda.*
Landiers	lah(n) **DYAY**	*(Fr.) Andirons*
Langue de Boeuf	lahng duh bu(r)f	*(Fr.) In armor, a 16th century pole arm whose blade resembled an ox's tongue.*
Lang Yao	lahng yow	*(Chi.) See Sang de boeuf*
Languedoc	lahng "**DOCK**" lah(n)g "**DUCK**" lang wuh "**DOCK**"	*(Fr.) A style of furniture named for this province in southern France. Also, a scarlet-colored French marble.*
Lannuier, Charles Honoré	lan wee **AY** shahrl oh noh **RAY**	*An American furniture-maker (1779-1819).*
Lapis Lazuli	**LAP** is **LAZ** oo lee **LAP** is **LAZ** oo lie	*A deep-blue semi-precious stone used for jewelry.*
Laristan Rug or Looristan	la ree **STAN** la ree **STAHN** **LOO** ris tan	*An oriental rug of Persian origin.*

L

La Rochelle	lah roe "**SHELL**"	(Fr.) A faïence factory founded in 1749 at La Rochelle, Charente-Inférieure.
Latticinio	lad uh **CHEEN** yoh lah tee **CHEEN** yoh	(It.) A clear glass decorated with embedded opaque white rods forming a pattern.
Laub und Bandelwerk	lowp oont bahnd'l vairk	(Ger.) Leaf and strapwork; ornamental motifs found on ceramics, glass, etc.
Laurier Aromatique	luhr **YAY** ah ruh mah **TEEK**	A hard, reddish-yellow wood of the oleander tree from the East Indies.
Lavabo	luh **VAH** boe la va **BOH**	(Fr.) A washstand.
Lavaliere	lah vuh **LEER**	A pendant ornament worn on a chain around the neck.
Layette	lay **ET**	(Fr.) In furniture, a small wooden coffer.
Lebes	**LEE** beez **LEH** ves	(Gk.) An ancient wine bowl without handles. Also, an ancient cauldron.
Le Corbusier	luh "core" boo **ZYAY**	Pseudonym for Charles-Edouard Jeanneret; architect and designer of furniture (1887-1965).
Le Creusot	luh crew **ZOH**	(Fr.) An 18th century glass factory originally founded near Sèvres.
Lei	lay^{ee}	(Chi.) A type of drinking vessel.
Lei Wen	lay^{ee} "one"	(Chi.) An archaic ornamental theme; "thunder pattern".

Lekane	**LEK** uh nee leh **KAH** neh *pl.* -nie	*(Gk.) An ancient Greek large bowl or basin-shaped vessel.*
Lekythos	**LEK** uh thahs **LEH** kee thohs *pl.* -"thigh"	*A Greek oil or perfume jar.*
Les Islettes	lay zees **LET**	*(Fr.) A faïence factory founded in 1785 at Bois d'Epense, near Lunéville.*
Lesum	**LAY** zum	*(Ger.) A faïence factory founded in 1785 at Lesum, near Bremen.*
Ley	lay	*A type of pewter of 80% tin and 20% lead.*
Li	lee	*(Chi.) A Bronze Age vessel.*
Liège	lezh	*(Fr.) Glass factories established during the late 16th century in and around Liège.*
Lien Tzu	lee en ds uh	*(Chi.) A type of footed bowl.*
Lierne	lee "**URN**"	*In architecture, a short rib.*
Lignum Vitae	**LIG** num **VIDE** ee **LIG** num **VITE** ee	*A very hard brown or greenish-black wood from South America.*
Lilihan	lee lee ahn	*A modern type of oriental rug of Persian origin.*
Lille	leel	*(Fr.) Faïence factories begun in Lille in the late 17th century onward. Also, a center for lace-making and tapestries.*
Limbach	lim bahk	*(Ger.) A porcelain factory founded at Limbach, Thuringia in 1772.*

L

Limner	**LIM** nur	An anonymous painter, usually with little formal training, of the American colonial period.
Limoges	lee "**MOW**"ZH	(Fr.) A faïence factory begun at Limoges in 1736. Also, a hard paste porcelain factory established in 1771.
Limousin	lee moo **ZA(N)**	(Fr.) A style of Provincial furniture named after a former province in central France.
Ling Chih	leeng j^{uh}	(Chi.) 'Magic mushroom' ornament. A symbol of long life and prosperity.
Ling Lung	leeng lohng	(Chi.) Referring to the delicate pierced or openwork found in ceramics.
Liseuse	lee **ZU(R)Z**	(Fr.) An 18th century reading table.
Lisieux	lee **ZYU(R)**	(Fr.) A tile-making faïence factory of the mid-17th century. Tiles were known as 'carreaux de Lisieux'.
Lit à Barreaux	lee ah ba **ROE**	(Fr.) A type of early 19th century bed having a low headboard.
Lit à Colonnes	lee ah kuh **LUN**	(Fr.) A tall postbed supporting a canopy or tester.
Lit à Couronne	lee ah koo **RUN**	(Fr.) A characteristic crown-shaped canopy found on a lit en bateau.
Lit à la Duchesse	lee ah lah due **SHESS**	(Fr.) A type of bed introduced in the late 17th century having a low headboard.
Lit à la Polonaise	lee ah lah puh luh **NEZ**	(Fr.) A type of bed whose head and footboard are of equal height.

Lit à la Turque	lee ah lah **TURK**	(Fr.) A type of bed placed against the wall lengthwise.
Lit à l'Impériale	lee ah la(m) "pair" **YAL**	(Fr.) A type of postbed.
Lit Clos	lee **KLOE**	(Fr.) A panelled wood bed popular in Brittany.
Lit d'Ange	lee **DAH(N)ZH**	(Fr.) A type of bed having a tester, but without posts.
Lit d'Anglais	lee dah(n) **GLAY**	(Fr.) A type of bed placed against the wall lengthwise.
Lit Demi-Clos	lee duh mee-**KLOE**	(Fr.) A panelled wood bed made without doors. See Lit Clos.
Lit de Parade	lee duh pah **RAHD**	(Fr.) A type of bed with elaborate curtaining and canopy.
Lit de Repos	lee duh ruh **POE**	(Fr.) A daybed or couch.
Lit en Bateau	lee ah(n) ba **TOE**	(Fr.) A boat-shaped bed.
Lit en Tombeau	lee ah(n) to(m) **BOE**	(Fr.) A type of tester bed.
Lit Jumeaux	lee zhoo **MOE**	(Fr.) Twin beds.
Lithophane	**LITH** uh fane	Porcelain having an intaglio decoration made distinct by transmitted light.
Lladró	yah **DROE** yah **THROH**	(Sp.) A ceramic factory founded by Juan José and Vicente Lladró in 1951 at Almacera. In 1958 it relocated to Tabernes Blanques.
Lochaber	lahk **AH** ber	A 16th century Scottish battle-ax.
Loc María	lohk mah **REE** ah	(Fr.) A faïence factory established in 1690 at Loc María near Quimper.

L

Loetz, Witwe	**LU(R)TS, VIT** vuh	(Aus.) A type of iridescent art glass made by Loetz Witwe glasshouse in the late 19ᵗʰ century
Loggia	**LAH** gᵉᵉuh **LOHD** jah	(It.) A veranda or portico projecting from a building.
Lohan	**"LOW"** hahn	In Chinese ornament, a Buddhist immortal.
Loredo Chiaro	loh **REH** doh **KYAH** roh	(It.) A light coffee-colored Italian marble.
Lorgnette	lor **NYET**	(Fr.) A pair of eye glasses or opera glasses attached to a handle.
Lorraine	luh **REN**	(Fr.) A style of furniture named after a French province. Also, a lace-making province.
Louis Quatorze	loo ee ka **TORZ**	(Fr.) A style of decoration during the reign of Louis XIV (1643-1715).
Louis Quinze	loo ee **KA(N)Z**	(Fr.) A style of decoration during the reign of Louis XV (1715-1774).
Louis Seize	loo ee **SEZ**	(Fr.) A style of decoration during the reign of Louis XVI (1774-1792).
Loutrophoros	loo **TRAHF** uh rahs loo troh **FOH** rohs	(Gk.) An ancient elongated water jar.
Louvre	loove loovrᵘʰ	(Fr.) Formerly a royal palace in Paris. Since 1793, a national museum.
Lowestoft	**LOWZ** tahft	A porcelain factory founded in 1757 at Lowestoft, Suffolk, England.
Lozenge	"lozenge"	In heraldry, a diamond-shaped figure.

Lucchese Patterns	loo **CHEH** zeh	*(It.) Patterns designed by the Lucchese weavers of the 13th and 14th century in the town of Lucca.*
Ludwigsburg	lood veeks boorg	*(Ger.) An important 18th century porcelain factory established at Ludwigsburg, Württenburg.*
Lu-hsing	loo-sheeng	*(Chi.) A Taoist deity.*
Lunel Uni	lu nel oo **NEE**	*A variety of marble quarried in northern France.*
Lunette	lu **NET**	*(Fr.) A semicircular or crescent-shaped window or panel.*
Lunéville	lu nay **VEEL**	*(Fr.) A faïence factory established at Lunéville in 1731.*
Lyonnais	lee uh **NAY**	*(Fr.) A style of furniture named after a province in east central France.*
Lyons	"lions" lee **OH(N)**	*(Fr.) A faïence center here from the 16th century onward. Also, silk factories flourished from the early 18th century to the present time.*

M

Maastricht	mahs tree<u>h</u>t	(Dut.) Faïence factory established in 1836 by Petrus Regout, and still in existence.
Mabe Pearl	mayb **MAH** "bee"	A form of cultured pearl.
Macassar Wood or Makassar	muh **KAS** er	A striped wood from the ebony tree in the Dutch East Indies.
Macchiaioli	mah kyah **YOH** lee	(It.) A group of 19th century Florentine artists whose work was fanciful rather than naturalistic, and characterized by blobs or patches of color.
Macchia	**MAH** kyah	(It.) Sketch or outline.
Machicolation	muh "**CHICK**" uh **LAY** shun	Openings in the floor beneath a parapet supported on corbels through which missiles were hurled onto an enemy.
Ma-Chün	mah-j^{ue}een	(Chi.) Early type of ceramic ware with finely crazed opaque glaze.
Macramé	**MACK** ruh may mack ruh **MAY**	A technique of decorative knotting.
Madeira Work	muh **DEER** uh muh **DEE** ruh	Pertaining to the needlework done on the island of Madeira.
Madia	**MAHD** yah	Italian Renaissance bread cupboard.
Maenad	**ME** nad	A priestess of Dionysus.

Maestà	mah es **TAH**	(It.) A painting of the Madonna and Child enthroned and supported by angels.
Magdeburg	mahk duh boork	(Ger.) A faïence factory founded at Magdeburg, Hanover in 1754.
Magot	mah **GO**	(Fr.) A grotesque figure seen on oriental porcelain. Also, 19th century Chinese and Japanese export wares regarded as distasteful.
Mahal Rug	muh **HAHL**	A Persian rug from the Sultanabad weaving area.
Maidou Wood	"my" **DOO**	A dark brown wood from Burma and Indonesia.
Maie	meh	(Fr.) A kneading trough.
Main Gauche	ma(n) gohsh	(Fr.) A 17th century left-handed dueling dagger.
Maître Banc	mehtr^{uh} bah(n)	(Fr.) A type of high back wooden bench.
Maître Ébéniste	mehtr^{uh} ay bay **NEEST**	(Fr.) A master cabinetmaker.
Majolica	mah **JO** lee kah muh **JAH** luh kuh	Any Italian tin-glazed, low-fired earthenware.
Majorelle, Louis	mah zhoh **RELL**, loo **EE**	A noted French furniture designer (1859-1926).
Makatlik	mah "cot" **"LICK"**	A Perso-Turkish word for a runner.
Makimono	mah kuh **MOE** no	A Japanese horizontal scroll painting designed to be unrolled.
Makkum Potteries	**MAH** kum	(Dut.) A faïence factory established in 1675 at Makkum in Friesland.

M

Makri *also* Melas	mahk ree	An oriental rug of Turkish origin.
Maksoorah	mac "**SUE**" rah	In a mosque, a screen or partition.
Malachite	**MA** luh "kite"	A green mineral often used for ornamental purposes.
Málaga Potteries	**MAH** lah gah	(Sp.) An early pottery district, known for the production of Hispano-Moresque Ware.
Malerisch	**MAH** luh reesh	(Ger.) A term meaning painterly or in a painterly manner.
Maline	muh **LEAN**	A delicate open mesh net resembling tulle.
Maltese Cross	"mall" **TEEZ** "mall" **TEES**	An eight-pointed cross.
Mamelières	mam l^{ee} "**AIR**"	(Fr.) 14th century circular plates of metal fastened on a knight's breastplate.
Mamori Katana	mah moh lee kah tah nah	(Jap.) The first sword given to a samurai boy.
Mamluk	**MAM** "luke"	A type of Egyptian carpet.
Manchette	mah(n) **SHET**	(Fr.) An armpad. Also, a term referring to a padded crest rail.
Mandala	**MUN** duh luh	A schematized representation of the cosmos used in Eastern religions.
Mandorla	**MAHN** "door" lah	(It.) In painting, an almond-shaped glory.
Manière Criblée	man **YAIR** creeb **LAY**	(Fr.) See Criblé

Manisses or Manises	mah **NEE** sehs	(Sp.) In ceramics, a 15th century center for luster-painted ware founded in this suburb of Valencia.
Mansard	**MAN** sahrd	A roof having two slopes on all sides, the lower one steeper than the upper slope.
Manteau	mah(n) **TOE**	(Fr.) A mantelshelf.
Mantua	**MAN** "chew" uh	The oldest Italian tapestry weaving center, from the 15th century onward.
Maquette	mah **KET**	A small preliminary model.
Marans	muh **RAN** ma **RAH(N)**	(Fr.) A 17th century faïence factory founded at Marans, Charente-Inférieure.
Marchepied	"marsh" **PYAY**	(Fr.) A term for a step, pair of steps or a footstool.
Marouflage	**MAHR** uh flahzh mahr uh **FLAHZH**	A process of attaching a painted canvas to a wall with acrylic binders.
Marquetry	**MAHR** kuh tree	A decorative veneer on furniture using small pieces of wood, shell, ivory, etc.
Marquise	mahr **KEEZ**	(Fr.) A deep upholstered armchair, wide enough for two. Also, a sheltered projection over an entrance.
Marronnier Wood	ma run **YAY**	(Fr.) A white-colored wood, both hard and soft, of the French chestnut tree.
Marseillemuster	mahr suh lay mu(r) "stair"	(Ger.) In porcelain, a type of molded ornament introduced in Meissen in the 1750's, used for the decoration of plates.

M

Marseilles Potteries	mahr **SAY**	*(Fr.) A faïence center at Marseilles beginning in the late 17th century.*
Marsulipatam	mar **SOO** leh pa tam	*See Masulipatum*
Maru-Bori	mah loo-boh lee	*(Jap.) A term for carving in the round.*
Maruyama School	mah loo yah mah	*(Jap.) An 18th century school noted for its realistic approach to painting.*
Mascaron	**MASK** uh rahn mas ka **ROH(N)**	*(Fr.) In architecture, a mask or grotesque figure.*
Mashiko	mah shee koh	*A handcrafted pottery center in Mashiko, Japan.*
Mashrebeeyah	mah shree **BEE** yah	*A latticed window.*
Mastaba	**MAST** uh buh	*An ancient Egyptian burial chamber. Also, a built-in seat or bench.*
Masulipatam Rug or Marsulipatam	ma **SOO** leh pa tam	*Oriental rugs woven in Masulipatam in southern India.*
Mathildenhöhe	mah **TEEL** d'n "her"yuh	*(Ger.) The artist colony of Mathildenhöhe-Dormstadt, founded by the Grand Duke Ernst Ludwig of Hesse-Dormstadt in 1899.*
Mauri	**MWAH** ree	*See Mori*
Maximinenstrasse	**MAHX** ee **MEE** nun **SHTRAH** suh	*(Ger.) One of the three principal stoneware manufactories in Cologne during the 16th century.*
Mayan	"my" yun	*Pertaining to a pre-Columbian civilization of the Yucatán Peninsula.*
Mazarine	ma zuh **REEN**	*A strainer fitting over a silver meat dish. Also, a deep rich blue color.*

Maze-Gane	mah tzeh-gah neh	(Jap.) A form of metal art.
Mazer	"**MAZE**" ur	A type of metal drinking vessel, formerly of wood.
Mechlin Lace	**MEK** lin	A fine Flemish bobbin-made lace with raised cord.
Médaillier	may dah **YAY**	(Fr.) A cabinet for the display of medals.
Medici	**MED** uh chee	Soft paste porcelain made under the protection of Francesco Maria de Medici between 1575 and 1587. Also, a 16ᵗʰ century Italian tapestry factory founded in Florence.
Medieval	mee dee **EE** vul mee **DEE** vul	A characteristic style of art and architecture produced in the Middle Ages in Europe mid-(500-1500).
Meerschaum	"**MERE**" shum "**MERE**" shawm	A mineral used for ornamental carvings.
Meiji	meh ee jee	A Japanese time period (1868-1912).
Meillonas	meh yoh **NAH**	(Fr.) A faïence factory established in 1759 near Bourg-en-Bresse.
Mei P'ing	may peeng	(Chi.) A Chinese vase with small neck and mouth, intended to hold a flowering prunus branch.
Meissen	"**MICE**" 'n	(Ger.) A porcelain factory founded at Meissen, near Dresden in 1710.
Mélange	may **LAH(N)ZH**	In jewelry, pertaining to the classification of diamonds.
Mélange Campan	may **LAH(N)ZH** ca(m) **PAH(N)**	A type of marble found in the Hautes-Pyrénées district in France.

M

Melas Rug	**MEH** lahs	*See Makri*
Mêlée	may **LAY**	*In jewelry, pertaining to the classification of diamonds.*
Mélèze Wood	may **LEZ**	*A hard, yellow-reddish wood of the larch tree.*
Ménager	may na **ZHAY**	*(Fr.) A buffet-vaisselier called ménager in Champagne.*
Mennecy	men **SEE**	*(Fr.) A porcelain factory founded at Paris in 1734, and later transferred to Mennecy and Bourg-la-Reine. Also called Mennecy-Villeroy.*
Mennecy-Villeroy	men **SEE**-veel **RWAH**	*See Mennecy*
Menorah	muh **NOR** uh muh **NO** ruh	*(Heb.) A candelabrum; a seven-branched sanctuary lamp.*
Mentonnière	mah(n) tun **YAIR**	*(Fr.) In armor, a tilting breast-plate for protecting the lower part of the face; an extra piece worn over the regular armor in tournaments.*
Menuisier	muh nwee **ZYAY**	*(Fr.) A maker of joined furniture.*
Menuki	meh noo kee	*(Jap.) Ornaments placed on the sides of the hilt of a Japanese knife or sword.*
Merese	may **REEZ**	*A flat, sharp-edged knop between the bowl and base of a drinking glass.*
Méridienne	may ree **DYEN**	*(Fr.) A daybed of the Empire period having arms of unequal height with a back panel.*
Merisier Wood	muh ree **ZYAY**	*A hard, reddish-striped wood of the wild cherry tree.*

Mesail	"MESS" "ale"	In armor, the movable visor found on medieval pig-faced bassinets.
Meshed	meh SHED	An oriental rug of Persian origin.
Métier	may TYAY	(Fr.) In art, the specialty of the artist or craftsman.
Metoche	"MET" "o" kee	In the Ionic order, the space between the dentils.
Metope	med OPE meh TOPE MED uh pee	The space between the triglyphs in the Doric frieze.
Meubles	MU(R) bl^uh	(Fr.) The term for movable furniture.
Meubles de Luxe	...duh LOOX	(Fr.) Luxurious furniture built more for show than for use.
Meubles Précieux	..."pray" SYU(R)	(Fr.) Objects made primarily for their decorative value. Popular during the second half of the 18th century.
Meubles Régionaux	...ray zhyun OH	(Fr.) Regional furniture.
Meubles Rustiques	...rue STEEK	(Fr.) Rustic furniture.
Mezzo-Rilievo	MET so-ree "LEAVE" oh MET soh-ree lee EH voh	(It.) Relief sculpture in which figures project half their proper proportion.
Mezzotint	MET so "tint"	(It.) A form of relief print made on a metal plate in which the artist works from dark to light.
Mianeh	mee AN ay	Persian runners made in the Hamadan style.
Mignonette	min yuh NET	A French bobbin lace.

Mihrab or Mirab	**MEE** rub "**MARE**" ab	A prayer niche which indicates the direction of Mecca.
Milch Glass	milk milch milks	Opaque white glass made as a substitute for porcelain.
Mildner Glass	meeld nur	(Ger.) A type of decorated glass.
Millefiori Glass	"mill" uh fee "**O**" ree mee leh **FYOH** ree	(It.) Ornamental glass technique, usually of a floral pattern.
Millefleurs	meel **FLUR**	(Fr. 'thousand flowers') An overall decorative motif of flowers.
Mina Khani Motif	**MEE** nah h̲ah nee	A type of repeated pattern used especially in Persian rugs.
Minaret	min uh **RET** **MIN** uh ret	A tall tower attached to a mosque from which the muezzin calls the people to prayer.
Mingei	meen gheh ee	Japanese folk art.
Mino Potteries	mee no	A center of Japanese potteries founded in the early 17th century, north of Nagaya.
Minoan	mi "**NO**" un	Pertaining to the ancient art and civilization of the island of Crete (3000-1000 B.C.).
Mir	meer	An oriental rug of Persian origin generally referred to as Mir Serebend. Also, a repetitive design of small botehs.
Mir Serebend Rug	meer "**SARAH**" bend	An oriental rug of Persian origin.
Mirzapore Rug or Mirzapur	**MEER** zuh "poor"	An oriental rug woven in Mirzapore, India.

Miserere	**MIZ** uh **REH** ree	In ecclesiastical furniture, a type of seat used during Catholic Church services for the aged and infirmed ecclesiastics.
Misericord	"misery" "cord"	A small seat placed within the church stall.
Miséricorde	mee zay ree "**CORD**"	A medieval dagger.
Mishima	mi **SHEE** muh **MEE** shee mah	In ceramics, a decorating technique originating in Korea.
Miter or Mitre	"**MY**" tur	The official headdress worn by bishops in the Western Church.
Mitokoromono	mee toh koh loh moh noh	(Jap.) In Japanese sword mounts, the term means 'objects for three places'—kogai, kozuka, and menuki.
Modello	moh **DEL** loh	(It.) A model; a sketch of a more finished model.
Moiré	"**MORE**" ay mwah **RAY**	Any silk or other fabric having a watery or wave-like appearance.
Mokko	moh koh	(Jap.) A Japanese tsuba having four lobes.
Mokkotsu	moh koh tsoo	(Jap.) A traditional ink painting with color.
Mo-Ku	moe-goo	(Chi.) In art, a picture painted freely with no lines being used.
Mokume-Ji	moh koo meh-jee	(Jap.) A Japanese metal art resembling wood graining.
Moline	**MOE** lin	In heraldry, a cross with forked arms.
Momoyama	moe moe yah mah	(Jap.) An historical period (1573-1615).

M

Monatsbecher	moh nahts **BEH** "care"	(Ger.) A small cup, usually of silver.
Monstrance	**MAHN** struns	A vessel in which the consecrated host is exposed.
Montage	mahn **TAHZH** moh(n) **TAHZH**	(Fr.) A picture made by overlapping or blending other pictures, photos, etc.
Montauban	moh(n) toe **BA(N)**	(Fr.) A faïence factory established here in 1761.
Monteith	**MAHN** "teeth" mahn "**TEETH**"	A large punch bowl with a notched rim.
Montareau	moh(n) ta **ROE**	(Fr.) A ceramic factory founded in 1775 at Montareau, Seine-et-Marne.
Montpellier	moh(n) puh **LYAY**	(Fr.) A faïence center established here from the late 16th century onward.
Moquette	moe **KET**	(Fr.) A type of fabric woven in the same manner as velvet.
Morbidezza	"more" bee **DET** sah	(It.) In painting, a term which denotes the exaggerated delicacy and vivid rendering of the flesh.
Moresque	muh **RESK**	A style of ornament reflecting Spanish-Moorish influence.
Mori or Mauri	**MWAH** ree	(Afg./Pak.) A term used to describe modern rugs of Turkoman design.
Morion	**MOE** ree un	A 16th century open helmet.
Mosaic	moe **ZAY** ik	A decorative art process of cementing small colored pieces of stone, glass, etc. to a base.

Mosaïk	moh zah eek	(Ger.) A type of porcelain decoration using an enamelled scale pattern.
Mosbach	mohs bahk	(Ger.) A faïence factory founded in 1770 at Mosbach, Baden.
Mouchette	moo **SHET**	(Fr.) A French limestone.
Moulage	moo **LAHZH**	(Fr.) Making a cast or an impression from a natural or ready-made object.
Moulin	moo **LA(N)**	(Fr. 'mill') A small utensil used for grinding.
Moustiers Potteries	moo stee **AY**	(Fr.) An important center for faïence factories.
Moutesham Kashan or Motasham	**MOO** tay shahm kuh **SHAHN**	(Per.) Rugs from Kashan.
Mud	"mood"	(Per.) A rug name of the Khorasan group.
Mudéjar	moo "**DAY**" hahr moo **THEH** hahr	(Sp.) A decorative style evolved in Spain by Christian or Moorish craftsmen under Moorish influence.
Mudjur	**MOOD** jah	(Anat.) An oriental rug of Anatolian classification.
Muffineer	"**MUFFIN**" "ear" "muffin" "**EAR**"	A small caster for sprinkling salt or sugar.
Mühlenbecher	"**MEW**" len **BEH** "care"	A 17th century Dutch drinking vessel. Also called a wind-mill cup.
Mukade	moo kah deh	(Jap. 'centipede') A design often used on Japanese sword fittings and armor.

Mullion	"**MULL**" yun	A vertical stone or wooden bar between the lights of a window.
Münden Pottery	**MOON** d'n	(Ger.) A faïence factory founded in or before 1737, at Münden, Hanover.
Murier Wood	mure **YAY**	A soft white and yellow wood of the mulberry tree.
Muromachi	moo roe mah chee	(Jap.) An historical period (1338-1573).
Musashi	moo sah shee	(Jap.) A pottery center in the province of Musashi.
Muscadier Wood	mue skah **DYAY**	A hard red and light yellow wood of the nutmeg tree from the East Indies.
Muskabad	moshk ah bahd	An oriental rug of Persian classification.
Mutule	"**MEW**" chool	A projecting block beneath the corona of a Doric cornice which is similar to a modillion of other orders.
Myall Wood	"**MY**" all	A hard fragrant wood, reddish or purplish in color from the acacia tree in Australia.
Mycenaean Art	"**MY**" suh **NEE** un "my" **SEE** nee un	The art and civilization of Mycenae during the late Helladic period (2000-1100 B.C.).

N

Nabeshima Ware	nah beh shee mah	(Jap.) A pottery center at Okawachi, Hizen province, founded in the mid-17th century.
Nabis, les	nah **BEE**, lay	(Fr.) A group of late 19th century French artists who exhibited together and were influenced by Paul Gauguin.
Nacre	**NAY** kur na kr^uh	(Fr.) Mother-of-pearl.
Nailsea	**NAIL** sea	An English glasshouse founded in 1788 in Nailsea in the Bristol district.
Nain	nah **EEN**	A Persian rug weaving town.
Namazlik	nah mahz leek	(Tur.) A term meaning prayer rug.
Namban	nahm bahn	(Jap.) A popular design used for decorating sword fittings.
Nanako	nah nah koh	(Jap.'fish roe') A surface decoration used as a background on sword fittings.
Nantgarw	nahnt gah roo	An English porcelain factory founded at Nantgarw, South Wales in 1813.
Naos	**NAY** ahs **NAH** ohs pl. -oy	In architecture, a temple, or inner chamber of a temple.

N

Narghile or Nargileh	**NAHR** guh lee **NAHR** guh leh	A Middle Eastern smoking pipe.
Nashi-Ji	nah shee jee	(Jap.) A lacquer work sprinkled with gold to resemble the skin of a pear.
Naumachia	naw **MAY** kee uh	An ancient Roman spectacle representing a sea-fight. Also, a place (e.g., amphitheatre, circus) for presenting such spectacles.
Nebris	**NEB** ris	A fawn skin worn in Greek mythology.
Nebuchadnezzar	neh buh "cud" **NEZ** zur	A 20 quart wine bottle.
Nephrite	**NEH** "fright"	A variety of jade.
Nereid	"**NEAR**" ee id	In Greek mythology, any of the 50 daughters of Nereus, a sea-god of Greece.
Nereus	"**NEAR**" ee "us" "**NEAR**" yoos	One of the sea-gods of Greece and father of the Nereids.
Netsuke	**NETS** kee **NET** skay **NET** suh kay	(Jap.) Small sculptured figures of ivory, wood, metal, or porcelain first used as toggles.
Neue Sachlichkeit	noy ᵞᵘʰ sahh leeh "kite"	(Ger.) A style of painting that developed in Germany in the 1920's as a reaction to expressionism and impressionism.
Neustadt-Eberswalde	noy shtaht-ay bairs vahldᵘʳ	(Ger.) A ceramic factory founded at Neustadt Eberswalde around 1799.
Nevers	nuh **VAIR**	(Fr.) A pottery center from the second half of the 16ᵗʰ century. Also, a glasshouse established there after 1566.

Niche	nish	A recess in a wall for holding a statue or ornament.
Niello	**NYEL** low	A technique of filling incised decorations on gold or silver with a black inlay.
Nihilism	"**NIGH**" uh liz um	In art, an anti-establishment revolt against existing values and smugness. See Dada.
Niku-Bori	nee koo-boh lee	(Jap.) Carving in relief.
Niobe	"**NIGH**" o bee	In Greek mythology, the daughter of Tantalus.
Niris	nay reez	An oriental rug of Persian origin.
Nishiki-e	nee shee kee-eh	(Jap. 'brocade picture') A variety of Japanese print using a wide range of colors.
Nishiki-de	nee shee kee-deh	(Jap.) A form of porcelain made in Arita, characterized by elaborate over-all designs.
Non Pareil	**NAHN** puh rel noh(n) pa **RAY**	In printing, a six-point type.
Noir Fin Marble	nwahr fa(n)	A Belgian marble having a deep black ground.
Nouveau Réalisme	noo **VOE** ray ah leez m^{uh}	(Fr. 'New Realism') The term used to describe work done by a group of French artists, similar to American pop art.
Nove	**NO** vay	(It.) Faïence and porcelain factories established at Nove, Venezia in the early 18th century.

N

Novyi	noh **WEE**	*(Rus.) An early 19th century porcelain factory founded at Kuziaevo, near Moscow by the three Novyi brothers.*
Numone-Zōgan	noo moh neh-zoh gahn	*(Jap.) A form of Japanese inlay work.*
Nuppen	**NOO** p'n	*(Ger.) A term for an ornamental drop of glass applied to the surface of a vessel.*
Nuppenbecher	**NOO** p'n **BEH** "care"	*(Ger.) A drinking glass decorated with applied drops of glass.*
Nuraghe	noo **RAH** "gay"	*A prehistoric Sardinian stone structure.*
Nurnberg	nurn bairk	*(Ger.) A faïence factory established here in 1712.*
Nymphaeum	nim **FEE** um *pl.* -uh	*An area having statuary, fountains, flowers, etc. Also, a Roman house of pleasure.*
Nymphenburg	**NEEM** fun **BOORG**	*(Ger.) A porcelain factory established at Neudeck in 1747 and moved to Nymphenburg in 1761.*
Nyon	nee **OH(N)**	*A Swiss porcelain factory established in Nyon near Geneva around 1780.*

O

Obanoh	oh bahn	*(Jap.) A print measuring 15" X 10".*
Obeche Wood	o "**BEE**" chee	*A hard, white to pale yellow wood from West Africa.*
Obelisk	**O** buh lisk	*A tall, tapering monolithic column.*
Obermaler	oh bair mah lair	*(Ger.) In 18th century German porcelain factories, the person in charge of the painting and design studios.*
Objet d'art	ohb zhay **DAHR**	*(Fr.) A term designating a work of art.*
Objet de vertu	ohb zhay duh vair **TUE**	*(Fr.) A term for a small art object of superb workmanship.*
Objet trouvé	ohb zhay troo **VAY**	*(Fr.'found object') An object presented unaltered as a work of art.*
Obsidian	ub **SID** ee un	*A hard volcanic glass usually red, green, or black in color.*
Oceanides	**O** see **AN** i deez	*In Greek mythology, any of the daughters of the sea-god Oceanus.*
Ochre or Ocher	**O** kur	*An earthy clay, yellow or reddish-brown in color, used as a pigment in paints.*
Ocrea	**AHK** ree uh	*In armor, a greave covering the leg below the knee.*

Oculus	**AHK** yuh lus *pl.* -lie	*In architecture, a circular* *opening or window.*
Odalisque	"**ODE**"^{ul} isk	*A female slave in a harem.*
Odeum	oh **DEE** um	*A public theater used* *principally for concerts.*
Odjaklik	oh jahk leek	*(Anat.) A small oriental rug. Its* *name denotes a hearth rug.*
Oeil-de-boeuf	ur-duh-**BURF** u(r)^{yuh}-duh-**BU(R)F**	*(Fr.'eye of an ox') A small* *circular window.*
Oeil-de-perdrix	ur-duh-pair **DREE** u(r)^{yuh}-duh-pair **DREE**	*(Fr.'eye of a partridge') A type of* *repetitive decoration seen* *mainly on Sèvres porcelain.*
Oenochoe or Oinochoë	ee **NOKE** oh ee oy **NOKE** oh ee ee no **HOH** ee	*(Gk.) An ancient wine jug.*
Oesterreichischer, Werkbund	**U(R)** stuh "**RYE**" "he" shuh **VAIRK** boond	*An Austrian organization founded* *in 1916, pertaining to the arts* *and crafts movement.*
Oettingen- Schrattengofen	**U(R)** t'n g'n- **SHRAH** t'n **HOPE** 'nat	*(Ger.) A faïence factory established in* *1735 Oettingen, Bavaria and moved* *to Schrattenhofen in 1737.*
Oeuvre	u(r)v r^{uh}	*(Fr.) The entire works of a given* *artist.*
Offenbach	**AH** fen **BAHK**	*(Ger.) A faïence factory estab-* *lished in 1739 at Offenbach near* *Frankfurt-on-Main.*
Ojime	oh jee meh	*(Jap.) A small bead used to* *tighten the suspension cord* *joining the netsuke to the inro.*
Okimon	ooh kee moh noh	*(Jap.) Ornaments which are* *more decorative than functional.*

Okochi	oh koh chee	*(Jap.) Kilns established at Okochi near Arita around 1660.*
Oliphant	**AH** luh funt	*A horn made from ivory.*
Olivier Wood	oh lee **VYAY**	*A hard wood of the olive tree, characterized by its yellow color with brown veins.*
Olpe	**OHL** pee	*(Gk.'leather jug') An ancient short-necked jug with no spout.*
Omuro	oh moo loh	*(Jap.) A kiln established at Omuro near Kyoto around the mid-17th century.*
Onager	"**ON**" uh jur	*An ancient military catapult which threw stones.*
Onocentaur	ah nuh **SEN** "tar"	*In mythology, a creature having a body part-human and part-ass.*
Onyx	**AH** nix	*A variety of quartz with alternate layers of color, usually black and white or brown and white.*
Opalescent	o puh "**LESS**" unt	*Having the iridescent colors like that of the opal.*
Opaque	o **PAKE**	*Not translucent or transparent.*
Opisthodomos	ah pus **THAH** duh mus oh pees **THOH** thoh mohs	*(Gk.) A room placed at the back of a temple.*
Opus Anglicanum	**O** pus an gluh **KUH** num	*English medieval church embroidery.*
Opus Tesselatum	...teh suh **LAHD** um	*Mosaic work using cubes in simple geometric motifs.*
Opus Vermiculatum	...vur mik yuh **LAHD** um	*Classical mosaic work employing very small stones. The wandering lines resemble worm-tracks.*

Orant	**OR** unt	A female figure with outstretched hands in a gesture of prayer.
Oreillettes	oh ray **"YET"**	(Fr.) In armor, ear guards, sometimes with a projecting spike, attached to the helmets of the 15th-16th century.
Orfèvrerie	"or" fev ruh **REE**	(Fr.) Jewlery composed mainly of gold or silver.
Oribe Ware	oh lee beh	(Jap.) A potteryware made by tea master Furuta Oribe (1544-1615).
Oriel	**OR** ee ul	In architecture, a bay window projecting out from a wall.
Oriflamme	**OR** uh flam oh ree **FLAHM**	(Fr.) The ancient royal red banner of France.
Orléans	or lay **AH(N)**	(Fr.) A faïence factory established at Orléans, Loiret in 1753.
Ormulo	**OR** muh loo	(Fr.'ground gold') Gilded bronze.
Orrery	**OR** uh ree	An apparatus for representing the motions and relative positions of the bodies in the solar system.
Orvieto	or vee **EH** toh	(It.) An early pottery center founded at Orvieto, Umbria in the 13th century.
Ossuary	**AHSH** uh "wary" **AHS** "u" "air" ee	A place or receptacle where the bones of the dead are kept.
Ottocento	ooh toh **CHEN** toh	(It.) Pertaining to the Italian art period of 1800-1900.
Ottomane	uh tuh **MAHN**	(Fr.) A type of upholstered couch or seat without a back.

Ottonian Art	ah "**TOE**" nee un	*Art or architecture produced in Germany during the Ottonian reign (919-1024).*
Ottweiler	**AHT** vie "lair"	*(Ger.) A faïence and porcelain factory founded at Ottweiler in 1763. Materials and molds transferred to Sarreguemines in 1794.*
Oubliette	oo blee **ET**	*(Fr.) A secret dungeon used in medieval times.*
Ouch	"ouch"	*In jewelry, an ornamental brooch or buckle.*
Oudenarde Tapestries	**OW** duh **NAHR** duh	*An important tapestry weaving center established at Oudenarde, Flanders in the 15ᵗʰ century.*
Oushak	**OO** "shack"	*See Ushak*
Ovolo	"**OVAL**" lo *pl.* -lee	*A convex quarter-round molding.*
Ozen	oh zen	*(Jap.) A lacquered tray.*
Ozier Pattern	"**OATS**" see ur	*(Ger.) In porcelain decoration, the repetitive relief border simulating basket-work as seen on Meissen tabelwares around 1735.*

P

Pa Chi Hsiang	bah jee sh^{ee}ahng	In Chinese art and symbols, the Eight Happy Omens.
Padouk Wood or Padauka	puh **DOWK**	A hard, rose-colored wood from Burma; kind of rosewood.
Pa Hsien	bah sh^{ee}en	(Chi.) Eight Taiost Immortals.
Paillasse or Palliase	pal **YASS** **PAL** yass	A small mattress of straw.
Pailoo	**"PIE"** "low"	·In Chinese architecture, a decorative gateway.
Paisley	**PAZE** lee	A type of soft woolen patterned fabric.
Pai Ting	"by" deeng	(Chi.) In ceramics, a name for the whiteware Northern Ting or white Ting.
Pai Tz'u	"by" ts^{uh}	(Chi.) In ceramics, a name for Blanc de Chine.
Paktong	**PAK** tong	An alloy of copper, zinc and nickel resembling silver.
Pa Ku	bah goo	In Chinese art, the name for a group of symbols.
Pa Kua	bah gwah	(Chi.) The eight Trigrams.
Palampore or Palampoor	**PAL** um par **PAL** um poor	A cotton print bedcover woven in different parts of India.

Palas	pah **LAS**	In rugs, a flatweave technique.
Palazzo	pah "**LOT**" "so" pah **LAHT** soh	(It.) A palace or any imposing building.
Palette	**PAL** it	In art, a flat board or tablet upon which colors are held and mixed.
Palier	pa **LYAY**	(Fr.) See Buffet-vaisselier; called a palier in Normandy.
Palimpsest	**PAL** imp sest	A parchment for writing on and erasing again.
Palissandre or Palisander	**PAL** uh sand ur	A hard reddish or purplish rosewood from Brazil.
Palissy ware	pa lee **SEE**	(Fr.) The glazed pottery made by Bernard Palissy (1510-90).
Palladian	puh **LAH** dee un puh **LAY** dee un	A style of architecture based upon the designs of Andrea Palladio (1518-80).
Pallette	**PAL** it	In armor, small metal plates fixed at the shoulder.
Palmette	**PAL** met	In ornament, a classical, fan-shaped palm leaf.
Palsjö	pahl "where"	(Swe.) A faïence factory established in 1765 at Palsjö, near Helsingborg.
Paludamentum	puh **LOO** duh **MUN** tum	In ancient costume, a cloak worn by the officials.
Pambe	**PAM** beh	(Per.) The word for cotton.
Pamuk	**PAM** ook	(Tur.) The word for cotton.

P

P'an	pahn	(Chi.) A type of basin for washing hands.
Panache	puh **NASH** puh **NAHSH** pa **NASH**	(Fr.) A bunch of feathers.
Pancarpi	"pan" "**CAR**" pee "**PAN**" "car" pee	(Gk.) A term for garlands of fruit, flowers, and leaves.
Panchetto	pahn **CHET** toe	(It.) A small, three-legged wooden side chair.
Panetière	pan **TYAIR**	A French Provincial livery cupboard, either hanging or standing.
Panier	pa **NYAY**	(Fr.) A hamper or basket.
Panoply	**PAN** uh plee	A decorative display or array of arms and armor.
Pantheon	**PAN** thee "on"	A temple dedicated to the gods.
Pan-t'o T'ai	bahn-toe "tie"	(Chi.) A delicate, eggshell-thin porcelain.
Pao-Pie	bow-b^{ee}eh	(Chi.) In ceramics, a type of spotted celadon.
Pa Pao	bah bow	(Chi.) In Buddhist symbols, the "Eight Treasures".
Pa-pei	bah-bay	(Chi.) A stem-cup.
Papelera	pah peh **LEH** rah	(Sp.) A cabinet used to hold documents and paper.
Papier-Mâché	"paper"-muh **SHAY** pa pyay-ma **SHAY**	(Fr.) Ground paper, usually mixed with glue, which can be molded.
Papiers Collés	**PAH** pyay **CAW** lay pa pyay cul **LAY**	(Fr.) Pictures created using papers cut and glued; a form of collage.

Papiers Déchirés	pa pyay day shee **RAY**	(Fr. 'tattered papers') Manipulated paper shapes attached to a background.
Pappenheimer	**PAH** pen "**HI**" mur	In arms, a 17ᵗʰ century type of rapier.
Papyrus	puh "**PIE**" rus	A writing material used by the ancient Egyptians, Romans and Greeks, prepared from the stem of an aquatic plant.
Parapet	**PAR** uh pit	A low wall or barrier along the edge of a roof or balcony.
Parergon	pa **RUR** gahn	In painting, a detail that is an accessory or embellishment to the main theme.
Parget	**PAHR** jet	An ornamental technique of coating plaster on walls or other surfaces.
Parian Ware	**PA** ree un	A type of white, hard paste porcelain, usually unglazed.
Parquet	pahr **KAY**	(Fr.) Flooring made of thin wood blocks arranged in geometrical designs.
Parquetage	pahr kuh **TAHZH**	(Fr.) Geometric patterns of inlaid wood.
Parquetry	**PAHR** kuh tree	A decorative surface of inlayed wood veneers.
Partizan	**PAHR** duh zun	A broad-bladed pole arm used throughout the 16ᵗʰ and 17ᵗʰ century.
Parure	puh **RURE**	A set of matching jewels or ornaments.
Pas d'Ane Guard	pah dahn	A pair of ring guards surrounding the blade of a medieval sword.

P

Passant	pa **SAH(N)**	A heraldic term for a beast walking with one forepaw raised.
Passement	"**PASS**" munt "pass" **MAH(N)**	An ornamental garment trimming of gold, silver or silk thread.
Passementerie	"pass" **MEN** tree "pass" mah(n) **TREE**	(Fr.) A garment trimming of lace, braid, beads, etc.
Passe-partout	"pass"-"par" **TOO**	(Fr.) A piece of decorative cardboard without a center used to mount a photograph or picture.
Passglas	**PAHS** glahs	(Ger.) A type of late 16th and 17th century green glass communal drinking vessel.
Pasticcio	pa **STEE** choe pahs **TEET** choh	(It.) See Pastiche.
Pastiche	pa **STEESH**	(Fr.) Borrowed styles combined to form a new work of art.
Pastiglia	pahs **TEE** lyah	(It.) A Renaissance surface decoration of molded plaster.
Pastille	pa **STEEL**	A crayon made of pastel.
Pastose	pa **STOSE**	A term describing thickly applied pigment.
Pâte de Riz	"pot" duh **REE**	(Fr.) A technique used to produce glass by firing glass powder in a mold.
Pâte de Verre	"pot" duh **VAIR**	(Fr. 'glass paste') An ornamental, usually colored glass, having the appearance of semi-precious stones.
Pâte Dure	"pot" "dure"	(Fr.) A term used for hard paste porcelain or "true" porcelain.

Pâte-sur-Pâte	"pot"-sur-"pot"	*(Fr. 'paste on paste') In ceramics, a process of using layers of slip to create a low relief decoration.*
Pâte Tendre	"pot" **TAH(N)** dr^{uh}	*(Fr.) Soft paste porcelain. An imitation of true porcelain.*
Paten	"Patton"	*A shallow metal plate for bread, used in the celebration of the Eucharist.*
Patera	**PAD** uh ruh *pl.* -ree	*A disk-like ornament.*
Patina	**PAD** uh nuh puh **TEE** nuh	*Surface effects on bronze produced by oxidation.*
Pavé	puh **VAY** pah **VAY**	*In jewelry, stones placed close together to conceal a metal base.*
Pavis	**PAV** iss	*A large, oblong medieval shield.*
Paysage	pay ee **ZAHZH**	*(Fr.) Landscape.*
Pectoral	**PEK** tur ul	*A covering worn on the breast for ornament or protection.*
Peintres de la Réalité, Les	**PA(N)** truh duh lah ray ah lee **TAY**, lay	*(Fr.) A 17th century group of French painters.*
Peinture à l'essence	pa(n) ture ah leh **SAH(N)S**	*(Fr.) In painting, when oil pigments have had the oil extracted with absorbent paper, then thinned with turpentine.*
Peinture claire	pa(n) ture **CLAIR**	*(Fr.) In painting, when a bright, flat color is placed next to a dark one to create form.*
Pelike	**PEL** i kee *pl.* -kie	*A pear-shaped storage jar with two handles.*

P

Pelmet	**PEL** mit	A decorative cornice or valance surrounding a window.
Piloti	pi "**LOT**" ee	Stilts of iron, steel, etc., to support a building above ground level.
Peony	"**PEA**" uh nee "pea" "**OWN**" ee	A flower representing spring in Chinese art.
Pensiero	pen **SYAIR** oh	(It.) A sketch.
Pentaptych	pen **TAP** "tick"	An altarpiece or work of art with five panels.
Pergola	**PUR** guh luh	A garden arbor.
Peridot	**PEH** ruh "doe" **PEH** ruh "dot"	A yellowish-green variety of olivine.
Périgord	pay ree **GOR**	(Fr.) Louis XIII cabinetwork made in the old division of the province of Guienne.
Peristyle	"**PAIR**" uh "style"	A colonnade surrounding a courtyard.
Perron	"**PAIR**" run "pair" **ROH(N)**	(Fr.) An outside platform in front of a building.
Persienne	"pair" **SYEN**	(Fr.) An outside window shutter.
Pesaro	peh **SAH** roe	(It.) Majolica potteries in Pesaro from the late 15th century onward.
Pétard	pay "**TAR**"	(Fr.'Fireworks') A term for a painting or sculpture wildly designed by color, arrangement, etc., to attract attention.
Petite	puh **TEET**	
Petite Commode	... kuh **MUD**	A small chest of drawers.

Petite Desserte	... day **SAIRT**	*(Fr.) A type of small serving table.*
Petite Rue Saint-Gilles	... rue sa(n) **ZHEEL**	*(Fr.) A hard paste porcelain factory founded at Paris in 1785.*
Petit-Pied	puh tee-**PYAY**	*(Fr.) A small stand.*
Petit Feu	puh tee **FU(R)**	*(Fr. 'little fire') Low-fired ceramics.*
Petit Point	ped ee "point"	*In needlework, a very small stitch on canvas.*
Petit Poussin	puh tee poo **SA(N)**	*(Fr.) An inexpensive bobbin lace.*
Pétrin	pay **TRA(N)**	*(Fr.) A kneading trough.*
Petroglyph	**PEH** truh glif	*A prehistoric image carved on rock.*
Petronel	**PET** ruh nul	*A type of firearm used from the 15th to 17th century.*
Petuntse	puh **TOON** tsuh "bye" **DUND** zuh	*In ceramics, a type of feldspar.*
Peuplier Wood	pu(r)p lee **YAY**	*A light, spongy white wood from the poplar tree.*
Pfalz-Zweibrücken	pfahltz-**ZVIE** "brew" k'n	*(Ger.) A Rhineland porcelain factory founded here in 1767.*
Phalera	**FAL** uh ruh *pl.* -ree/-rye	*Metal discs worn in ancient times on the heads or breasts of horses or sometimes by men, as signs of military rank.*
Pharos	"**FAR**" ahs **FAY** rahs	*In architecture, a Roman lighthouse.*
Phial	**FIE** ul	*A small container for liquids.*
Phiale	**FIE** uh lee fee **AH** lee	*(Gk.) A shallow cup without handles used as a drinking vessel.*

P

Phoenix	**FEE** niks	A mythological bird.
Phyfe or Phyffe	"fife"	A furniture style named after American cabinetmaker and designer Duncan Phyffe (1768-1854).
Phylactery	fi **LAK** tuh ree	A container enclosing a holy relic. Also, something worn as protection or a charm.
Piatraccia	pyah **TRAH** chee ah	(It.) A lightly-veined Italian marble.
Piazza	**PYAH** tsah	(It.) An open area or public place.
Picardy	pee kahr **DEE**	(Fr.) A style of French Provincial furniture named for an old province.
Picot	**PEE** koe	In lacemaking, one of a number of decorative loops.
Pied de Biche	pyay duh **BEESH**	In furniture, a type of foot used to terminate a cabriole leg, resembling a deer's hoof. Also, a term used for the trifid-end spoon in English silver.
Piédouche	pyay **DOOSH**	In architecture, a small pedestal used for supporting a bust.
Pien Hu	b^{ee}en "who"	(Chi.) A pilgrim flask.
Pietà	pee eh **TAH**	(It.) The representation of the dead Christ lying in the lap of the Virgin.
Pietra Dura	**PYEH** trah **DOO** rah	(It.'hard stone') A type of inlaid mosaic work using semi-precious stones.
Pilaster	pih "**LASS**" ter	A rectangular pier projecting from a wall.

P'ing	peeng	The Chinese name for a vase.
Pingsdorf	peenks dorf	(Ger.) A name given to a group of early unglazed Rhenish stoneware.
Pinte	**PIN** tuh	(Ger.) A type of Rhenish stoneware mug or tankard.
Piqué	pee **KAY**	In jewelry, a decorative inlay technique on tortoise shell or ivory using silver or gold. Also, a type of fabric or fine embroidery.
Piqué Assiette	pee kay "ass" "**YET**"	(Fr.) A folk art technique covering forms and objects; e.g., broken tile, mosaics, beads, buttons, etc.
Piqué d'Or	pee kay "**DOOR**"	(Fr.) A decorative technique in tortoise shell using gold nails or studs.
Piscina	pi "**SIGH**" nuh pi **SEE** nuh	A pierced basin used for certain ablutions. Also, a large, public water basin.
Pithos	**PI** thahs **PIE** thahs **PEE** thohs *pl.* -thoy	(Gk.) A large earthenware storage jar.
Pittura Metafisica	pee **TOO** rah meh tah **FEE** see kah	(It. 'metaphysical painting') A pseudo-surrealistic art style in Italy around 1915-1921.
Pittura Traslucida	pee **TOO** rah trahz **LOO** chee doh	(It.) In painting, the use of transparent colors over a metal surface.
Pi Yü	bee yue	(Chi.) A dark green variety of jade.
Placcate	"**PLACQUE**" it	A medieval piece of plate armor used as reinforcement over a breastplate.

P

Placet	pla **SEH**	(Fr.) A term used for a stool.
Plafond	pluh **FAHN** pla **FOH(N)**	(Fr.) A painting on a ceiling, usually of decorative character.
Plaque	plak	An ornamental or commemorative tablet for hanging on a wall.
Plaquette	pla **KET**	(Fr.) A smaller version of a plaque.
Plastron-de-Fer	pla stroh(n)-duh-"**FAIR**"	(Fr.) In armor, a type of medieval iron breastplate.
Platane Wood	plah **TAHN**	A soft brown wood from the plane tree.
Plateau	plah **TOE**	An ornamental centerpiece for the dining table.
Plateresque	plad uh **RESK**	The architecture and ornament of the early Spanish Renaissance period (late 15th-early 16th century). Also, the term referring to the ornamental silver and gold work produced during that period.
Plaue-on-Havel	plow[er]-ahn-**HAH** vul	(Ger.) A pottery factory founded at Brandenburg in 1713.
Plein Air	"plane" "**AIR**" plen "**AIR**"	(Fr. 'open air') The term refers to a painting executed out of doors.
Pleinairistes	"**PLAY**" na rists	A group of 19th century Impressionists who painted out of doors.
Plemochoë	plee "**MOCK**" "o" ee plee moh **HOH** ee pl. -"eye"	(Gk.) An ancient covered container for perfume. Also called a Kothon.
Plenum	**PLEE** num **PLEN** um	A space above the ceiling and below a floor used for utility conduits.

Plique-à-Jour	pleek-ah-**ZHOOR**	*(Fr.) An enameling technique resulting in a miniature stained-glass effect.*
Pnyxniks	p^{uh}neeks	*A hill in Athens, Greece, where people assembled.*
Pochade	puh **SHAHD**	*(Fr.) A type of rough sketch.*
Pochoir	puhsh **WAHR**	*(Fr.) Stencil.*
Poinçon	pwa(n) **SOH(N)**	*A pointed metallic instrument used to pierce hard material.*
Point	pwa(n)	
Point à l'Aiguille	...tah lay **GWEEL**	*(Fr.) A term for needlepoint lace.*
Point Appliqué	...tap plee **KAY**	*Needlepoint appliquéd to a net foundation.*
Point Coupé	...koo **PAY**	*(Fr.) A term for cut work and reticella.*
Point d'Alençon	...duh **LENN** sahn ...d"allen" sahn ...da lah(n) soh(n)	*(Fr.) See Alençon*
Point d'Angleterre	...dah(n) gluh **TAIR**	*(Fr.) A needlepoint or bobbin lace having a bobbinet ground.*
Point d'Argentan	...**DAHR** jun tan ...dahr zhah(n) **TAH(N)**	*(Fr.) See Argentan*
Point d'Arras	...da rah	*(Fr.) A close textured, inexpensive bobbin lace.*
Point de Bruxelles	...duh brue "**SELL**"	*(Fr.) See Angleterre*
Point de Gaze	...duh **GAHZ**	*(Fr.) A light needlepoint lace made in Belgium.*
Point de Neige	...duh **NEZH**	*(Fr.) A form of raised needlepoint having a snow-like design.*

P

Point de Paris	...duh pah **REE**	(Fr.) A type of narrow bobbin lace.
Point de Raccroc	...duh ra "**CROW**"	(Fr.) A special stitch used in lace-making.
Point d'Espagne	...deh **SPAN**ʸᵘʰ	(Fr.) Gold laces enhanced with colored silks.
Point d'Esprit	...deh **SPREE**	(Fr.) Tulle embroidered with solid dots.
Point de Tulle	...duh "**TOOL**"	(Fr.) A term used occasionally for mignonette lace.
Point de Venise	...duh vuh **NEEZ**	(Fr.) Fine needlepoint lace.
Point de Venise à Réseau	...duh vuh **NEEZ** ah ray **ZOE**	(Fr.) A fine linen Venetian point lace.
Point Double	...dooblᵘʰ	(Fr.) A synonym of Point de Paris.
Pointillé	pwa(n) tee **YAY**	(Fr.) A decorative technique on leather used especially on book covers. Also, an early technique decorating metal with small dots.
Point Plat	pwa(n) **PLAH**	(Fr.) Needlepoint with a flat design.
Point Plat de Venise	pwa(n) **PLAH** duh vuh **NEEZ**	(Fr.) Venetian point lace without any raised treatment.
Point Plat de Venise au Fuseau	pwa(n) **PLAH** duh vuh **NEEZ** oh fue **ZOE**	(Fr.) A contemporary Venetian lace made with bobbins.
Poirier Wood	pwahr **YAY**	A very hard reddish wood from the pear tree.
Poissarde	pwah **SAHRD**	A popular style of earring worn in late 19th century France.
Poitou	pwah **TOO**	(Fr.) Provincial furniture of Poitou, an old province in western France.

Pokal	**POH** kahl	(Ger.) A large standing covered wine goblet or cup.
Policheh	pol lee **CHAY**	A "standard-size" rug, approximately 7'X 4' (2.13 X 1.22 m.).
Polyptych	"**POLYP**" "tick" puh **LIP** "tick"	A picture or relief carving consisting of a number of panels fastened together.
Pomander	poe **MAN** der **POE** man der	A ball of aromatic substances enclosed in a container.
Pommel	**PUM** mul **PAHM** mul	The knob terminating the hilt of a sword or knife.
Pommier Wood	pum **YAY**	A hard white wood from the apple tree.
Pompeian	pahm **PAY** un pahm **PEE** un	Pertaining to paintings uncovered in Pompeii. Also, a style of furniture in the Neo-classic taste.
Pompier	poh(m) **PYAY**	(Fr.) In art, a term sometimes used to describe a garish or pretentious style.
Poniard	**PAHN** yerd	A type of small dagger.
Pont-aux-Choux	poh(n)-toe-"**SHOE**"	(Fr.) A mid-18th century Parisian factory producing white earthenware.
Ponteuse	poh(n) **TU(R)Z**	(Fr.) A type of 18th century chair.
Poppelsdorf	**POH** pulz **DORF**	(Ger.) A faïence factory founded in 1755 near Bonn.
Porphyry	"**PORE**" fuh ree	A hard rock, purplish-red or green in color, containing crystals of feldspar.

P

Porró	poh **ROH**	(Sp.) A spouted glass wine
Porrón	poh **ROHN**	vessel.
Porsgrund	pors grohn	(Nor.) A porcelain factory begun in 1887 and still in existence.
Portail	"pour" "**TAIL**"	A door; a gate; an entrance.
Portcullis	"port" "**CULL**" is	In medieval times, a strong iron grid for the gate of a castle or town.
Porte-Assiette	"port"-"ass" "**YET**"	(Fr.) A plate stand.
Porte-Cochère	"port"-cuh "**SHARE**"	(Fr.) A gateway through which a vehicle may pass.
Portico	"**POUR**" tee coh	(It.) A covered walk; a roof supported by columns.
Portière	"pour" **TYAIR**	(Fr.) A curtain made to hang over a door used as a decoration or concealment.
Posé d'Or	poh zay "**DOOR**"	(Fr.) A tortoise shell inlaid with chased gold motifs.
Posset Pot	**PAH** sit	An English ceramic drinking vessel for posset.
Potiche	poe **TEESH**	(Fr.) A porcelain or pottery jar of rounded or polygonal form.
Pot-Pourri	poe-"poor" **REE**	Aromatic leaves and petals kept in a jar.
Potschappel	"pot" "chapel"	(Ger.) A porcelain factory founded in the 1870's near Meissen.
Potsdam	pohts dahm	A glass manufactory founded in 1674 at Drewitz near Potsdam. Also, a faïence factory founded around 1739.

Pou	boe	*A Chinese covered ritual vessel.*
Poudreuse	poo **DRU(R)Z**	*(Fr.) A dressing table of the 18th century. Also called table à coiffeuse.*
Pouffe	poof	*An English term for a cushion-like seat.*
Poulaines	poo **LEN**	*(Fr.) Long-pointed shoes of the 15th century.*
Poupée, à la	poo "**PAY**", ah lah	*(Fr.) A technique of making several impressions from the same plate on color etchings or engravings.*
Poussinistes	**POO** see nists	*French painters of the 17th and 18th century who were followers of Poussin.*
Predella	preh **DELL** uh *pl.* -ee	*(It.) A step which projects beneath an altar -piece, often decorated with painted scenes or reliefs.*
Pre-Raphaelite	pre-"**RAFFLE**" ite	*A brotherhood of English artists formed in 1848.*
Presbytery	**PREZ** bi "terry"	*In architecture, that portion of the church reserved for the clergy.*
Prie-Dieu	pree-**DYU(R)**	*(Fr.) A small praying or kneeling stand. Also, an upholstered kneeling or praying chair.*
Pronaos	pro **NAY** ohs **PRO** nay ahs **PRO** nah ohs *pl.* -**NAY** oy	*(Gk.) In a classical temple, the portico or porch in front of the cella.*
Propylaeum	"**PROP**" uh **LEE** um *pl.* -uh	*The entrance gateway to a temple area.*

P

Proskau	**PROHS** "cow"	(Ger.) A faïence factory founded in 1763 at Proskau, Silesia.
Provence	pruh **VAH(N)S**	(Fr.) An old province and principal cabinetmaking center. Also, a style of furniture named for the province.
Prunier Wood	prue **NYAY**	A hard wood of the plum tree.
Prytaneum	**PRIT**un **EE** um	A public hall in ancient Greece.
Psalter	"**SALT**" ur	A printed book of Psalms.
Psaltery	**SAWL** tuh ree	An ancient stringed musical instrument.
Psyché	psee **SHAY**	(Fr.) A type of late 18th century mahogany cheval dressing glass.
Psykter or Psycter	**SIK** tur **PSEEK** teer	(Gk.) A pottery jar used for cooling wine.
Pteroma	tuh **ROE** muh *pl.* -mud uh	(Gk.) In classical architecture, the portico surrounding the cella of a temple.
Pteron	**TEH** rahn pteh **ROHN**	(Gk.) An external collonade, as in a Greek temple.
Puente Stand	**PWEN** tay	(Sp.) A carved table trestle stand.
Punch'ong	p"young" chung	(Kor.) A large class of ceramic ware from the early part of the Yi period (1392-1910).
Punjab	**PUN** jab	A district of northern India and Pakistan known for the cotton grown there.
Punto	**POON** toh	The Italian word for stitch. Also, laces in Spain.

Punto a Groppo	...ah "**GROW**" poh	(It.) A term for macramé; knotted stitch.
Punto a Maglia Quadra	...ah **MAH** lyah **KWAH** drah	(It.) Lace having a square mesh ground.
Punto a Relievo	...ah ree "**LEAVE**" oh	(It.) Stitches with raised work.
Punto d'Avorio	...dah **VOH** ryoh	(It.) A low relief needlepoint lace.
Punto Gotico	...**GO** tee koh	(It.) A 16th century lace with Gothic motifs.
Punto in Aria	...een **AH** ryah	(It.) An early needlepoint lace worked in buttonhole stitch.
Punto Tagliato	...tah **LYAH** toh	(It.) A term for cut work.
Punto Tagliato a Fogliami	...ah foh **LYAH** mee	(It.) The most intricate variety of Venetian point lace with elaborate raised work.
Punto Tirato	...tee **RAH** toh	(It.) A term for drawn work.
Purlin	"**PURR**" lin	In architecture, a transverse horizontal member in a roof frame for supporting the rafters.
Purree	"**POOR**" ee	In painting, a term for the pigment Indian yellow.
Pushmina	puhsh **MEE** nur	The wooly underhair of goats from northern India.
Pushti	"**PUSH**" tee	A Turkish term for the smallest sized rug, 3'X 2'(.91 X .61 m.).
Pu-Tai Ho-Shang	boo-die huh-shahng	A Chinese Buddhist god of children and earthly happiness.
Putto	"**PUT**" toh pl. -tee	(It.) A cherubic infant, often naked.

P

Pycnostyle	**PIK** neh **"STYLE"**	*In architecture, when space between columns measures one and a half times the diameter of one column.*
Pylon	**"PIE"** lahn	*In Egyptian architecture, an ancient massive gateway usually with flanking towers.*
Pyramidion	**"peer"** uh **MID** ee un	*A small pyramid.*
Pyre	**"PIE"**ur	*A pile of wood for burning a dead body.*
Pyrography	**"pie" RAHG** ruh fee	*The art of burning designs on wood by charring it with heated tools.*
Pyrope	**"PIE" "rope"**	*A variety of garnet, deep red in color.*
Pyx	**"picks"**	*The box or vessel for the sacred Host.*
Pyxis	**PIK** sis **PEEK** sees *pl.* **-PIK** suh deez	*(Gk.) A covered box used for toilet articles.*

Q

Quadriga	kwo **DREE** guh kwo "**DRY**" guh	A four-horsed chariot.
Quadrille	kwah "**DRILL**"	Paper ruled in squares.
Quadripartite	"quad" ruh "**PAR**" tite	Medieval ribbed or groined vaults consisting of four parts.
Quaich	"quake"	A Scottish shallow drinking bowl.
Quatrefoil	**KAD** er "foil" **KA** truh "foil"	In architecture, a Gothic tracery opening comprised of a four-lobed shape.
Quattrocento	**KWAH** troh **CHEN** toh	Pertaining to the Italian art period 1400-1500.
Quenouille	kuh **NOO**yuh	(Fr.) A bedpost; a turned wood support.
Quezal	kay **SAHL**	American Art Glass Co. that imitated Louis C. Tiffany's iridescent glass.
Quillons	kee **YOH**(**N**)	A sword guard.
Quimper	ka(m) "**PAIR**"	(Fr.) A faïence factory founded in 1690 at Loc Maria near Quimper.
Quintain	**KWIN** t'n	A wooden post used as a target in medieval military exercises.
Qum or Kum	ghoom	A Persian weaving center known for silk rugs.

| Quodlibetz | **KWAHD** luh bets | *In ceramics, a composition of articles; e.g., playing cards, scissors, etc. used as decoration.* |
| Quoin | "coin" | *In architecture, the external angle of a building.* |

R

Rabato or Rebato	ruh **BAH** toe	A wide, stiff collar of the 17th century worn by gentlemen.
Racinage	ra see nahzh	A decorative treatment of leather using acids to create patterns of leaves, twigs, etc.
Raeren Potteries	**RAY** rin	(Ger.) Potteries producing fine salt-glazed stoneware in the mid-16th century.
Raffia	**RAF** ee uh	Fiber obtained from the raffia palm; material used for weaving.
Rafraîchissoir	ruh "fresh" uh **SWAHR** ra "fresh" ee **SWAHR**	(Fr.) A wine cooler in the form of a small table.
Rais de Coeur	red kur	(Fr.) In architecture, a system of ornament in the form of a heart found on some moldings which have a convex profile.
Raku Ware	**RAH** koo	(Jap.) A thick-walled earthen-ware, used in the tea ceremony.
Ranseur	rah(n) **SUHR**	In armor, a pole arm consisting of a long cutting blade.
Raphaelesque	**RAH** fee uh **LESK**	A style of painting characteristic of, or pertaining to, the 19th century painter Raphael.
Rapier	**RAY** pee ur	A small, light sword with a narrow blade.

R

Rappoir	rah **PWAHR**	An 18th century file used as a tobacco grater, usually made of ivory or bone.
Ratskrug or Ratskanne	rahts kroog rahts kahn^{uh}	(Ger.) A type of stoneware jug.
Rattan	ra **TAN**	Tough stems of various climbing palms used for wickerwork.
Rauenstein	**ROW** en **SHTINE**	(Ger.) A porcelain factory founded in 1783 at Rauenstein, producing mostly imitation Meissen tablewares.
Rayère	reh **YAIR**	(Fr.) In architecture, the narrow opening in the wall of a medieval castle which admitted light.
Rebus	**REE** bus	A word represented by symbols or pictures.
Récamier	ray kuh **MYAY** ray ka **MYAY**	(Fr.) A daybed of the Directoire and Empire periods (1793-1830).
Réchampé	ray shah(m) **PAY**	(Fr.) A carved ornament crafted in gold or in a contrasting color.
Redan	ri **DAN**	In Gothic architecture, a system of ornament either pierced or indented.
Regardant	ruh gahr **DAH(N)**	In heraldry, an animal looking backwards.
Régence	ray **ZHAH(N)S**	(Fr.) Pertaining to the transitional style of furniture and decoration in France (1715-23).
Regensbur	gray "guns" boorg	(Ger.) A porcelain-decorating factory founded during the late 18th century in Regensburg, Bavaria.

Reglet	**REG** lit	*In architecture, a small flat molding.*
Regula	**REG** yuh luh *pl.* -lee	*In architecture, a reglet.*
Rehoboam	ree uh **BOE** um	*A large wine bottle.*
Reichenau School	**RIKE** uh "**NOW**"	*A German school of manuscript illuminators (965-1065).*
Reichsadlerhumpen	**RIKES AHD** lur **HOOM** p'n	*(Ger.) A glass cylindrical beaker and cover.*
Reims School	reems	*A French school of manuscript illuminators (8th-11th century).*
Reja	**RAY** <u>ha</u>	*(Sp.) A term for the iron grill of a window.*
Rilievo Schiacciato	ree "**LEAVE**" oh ree lee **EH** voh "ski" ah **CHAH** toe	*(It.) In sculpture, a flattened relief.*
Reliquary	**REH** luh **KWEH** ree	*A vessel or box in which relics are kept.*
Remarque	"remark"	*In etching, a small sketch in the margin of the plate.*
Renaissance	**REN** uh sahns ren uh **SAHNS**	*The revival of culture and learning in Western Europe during the 14th-16th century.*
Rendsburg	rents boork	*(Ger.) A faïence factory established in 1764 at Rendsburg, Halstein.*
Rennes	ren	*(Fr.) A pottery center in Rennes, Brittany from the 16th century.*
Repoussage	ruh poo **SAHZH**	*(Fr.) Flattening of the surface of an altered or repaired copper plate by hammering on the reverse side.*

Repoussé	ruh poo **SAY**	(Fr.) Relief designs on metal by hammering the reverse side.
Repoussoir	ruh poo **SWAHR**	(Fr.) An object or figure placed in the foreground of a picture to help direct the eye into the composition.
Rerebrace	"**REAR**" brace	A medieval plate armor for the upper arm.
Reredos	**REH** ruh dahs	An ornamental screen at the back of an altar.
Réseau	ray **ZOE**	(Fr.) A net; a meshed or netted ground resembling a network.
Réseau Rosacé	ray **ZOE** ro zah **SAY**	A lace ground.
Reseda	ruh **SEE** duh	A grayish-green color.
Resilla	ray **ZEE** yah	A hair covering comprised of a network of beads and secured by a comb.
Ressenti	reh **SEHN** tee	(It.) In art, a term denoting forcible expression.
Retable	ri "**TABLE**"	A shelf on which ornaments are placed; a frame which encloses decorated panels. Also, the altarpiece or panels themselves.
Retablo	ray **TAH** "blow"	A religious picture used as a votive offering.
Reticella	red uh **CHEL** luh	(It.) A decorative fabric. Also, a type of needlepoint lace.
Reticulated	ri **TIK** yuh lay ted	Decorated in a net-like arrangement.

Rétirage	ray tee **RAHZH**	(Fr.) In graphics, the pulling of a second print without having to re-ink the plate.
Retroussage	ruh troo **SAHZH**	(Fr.) In printmaking, the technique of bringing ink up from the lines in an intaglio plate.
Réveillon, Jean Baptiste	ray vay **YOH(N)** zhah(n) bap **TEEST**	(Fr.) An 18th century Parisian designer and wallpaper manufacturer.
Rheims Tapestries	reemz	Tapestry factories established at Rheims, France from the 15th century onward.
Rheinsberg	**"RHINES"** bairk	(Ger.) A faïence factory established in 1762 at Rheinsberg, Brandenburg.
Rhyton	**"RYE"** tahn ree **TOHN**	(Gk.) An ancient pottery drinking horn, the base usually shaped like an animal's head or mythological creature.
Rhodonite	**"ROAD"** 'n ite	A mineral used as an ornamental stone.
Ricasso	ree **KAH** so	In arms, the squared part of the rapier blade next to the hilt.
Rideau	ree **"DOE"**	(Fr.) A curtain or screen.
Rigaree	**RIG** uh ree	A type of applied decoration on glass.
Rinceau(x)	ra(n) **SO**	(Fr.) In ornament, a foliated or floral pattern.
Riobitsu	lee oh bee tsoo	In Japanese sword mounts, the openings in a tsuba for the kozuda and kogai.
Ritoccata	ree toh **KAH** tah	(It.) A term used for the area on a painting that has been retouched.

R

Rivière	riv ee "**R**" ree **VYAIR**	(Fr.) A necklace of gemstones usually of more than one strand.
Rocaille	roe **KIE**	(Fr. 'rockwork') An ornamental style based on shellwork and forms of rock, popular in 18th century France.
Rochet	**RAHCH** it	A garment resembling a surplice worn by bishops and abbots.
Rococo	ruh **KOH** koh roe kuh **KOH**	An 18th century style of art and interior decoration closely linked with the reign of Louis XV of France.
Roemer	**RU(R)** "mare"	(Ger.) A Rhenish wine glass.
Roirol	oh ee loh	(Jap.) A highly polished black lacquer.
Roman Breche	bresh	(Fr.) A French marble character-ized by mottled blues and pinks.
Romanesque	"roman" **ESK**	A transitional, pre-Gothic style of architecture and the decorative arts which prevailed in Western Europe from the end of the 8th century until the 12th century.
Rondache	rahn **DASH**	(Fr.) A medieval circular shield carried by foot soldiers.
Ronde-bosse	roh(n)d-"**BUS**"	(Fr.) A sculptured object in the round.
Rondelle	rahn **DELL**	A small piece of glass used in leaded windows.
Rörstrand	"roar" strahnd	(Swe.) A faïence factory begun in Rörstrand, near Stockholm, in 1725.

Rose Campan	kah(m) **PAH(N)**	*(Fr.) A pink and white variegated marble found in the Campan district, Haute-Pyrénées.*
Rose Point de Venise	pwa(n) duh vuh **NEEZ**	*Venetian raised point lace.*
Rose Pompadour	**POM** puh "door"	*(Fr.) A rose-pink opaque ground color used on porcelain at Sèvres around 1757.*
Rosetta Wood	roe **ZED** uh roe **ZEH** tuh	*A hard reddish-orange wood of the East Indies.*
Rosette	roe **ZET**	*(Fr.) A carved or painted rose-shaped ornament.*
Rosicrucians	**ROSE** uh **KROOSH** un **ROE** zi **KROO** shun	*A group of late 19th century Symbolist artists.*
Rosso Antico	**RO** so an **TEE** koh	*A type of unglazed red stoneware made by Wedgwood.*
Rosso Magnaboschi	**RO** so mah nyah **BOHS** kee	*An Italian red-colored marble.*
Rostrum	**RAHS** trum	*Any platform or stage used for public speeches. Also, a beaklike projection from the prow of an ancient ship.*
Rotogravure	roe tuh gruh **VYOOR** roe tuh "**GRAY**" vyoor	*A photomechanical intaglio printing method.*
Rotunda	roe **TUN** duh	*A circular building, usually one with a dome.*
Rouen	roo **AHN** roo **AH(N)**	*(Fr.) An important ceramic center for the production of faïence from the early 16th century.*
Rouet	roo **EH**	*(Fr.) Spinning wheel.*

R

Rouge Campan	roozh kah(m) **PAH(N)**	*(Fr.) A mottled red, violet and white variegated marble found in the Campan district, Hautes-Pyrénées.*
Rouge de Cuivre	...duh **KWEEVR**^{uh}	*A French name for an underglaze red used on Chinese ceramics from 1426-1435 (Hsüan Tê period).*
Rouge de Flandres Marble	...duh **FLAH(N)DR**^{uh}	*A Belgian red marble characterized by white veining.*
Rouge Jascolin	...zhas coh **LA(N)**	*An Italian marble with a red and cream-colored ground.*
Roulette	roo **LET**	*An instrument used for making dotted lines.*
Roundel	"**ROUND**" 'l	*In design, a circular decorative window or medallion. In armor, a small circular shield.*
Rubénisme	rue bay **NEEZ**^{muh}	*A late 17th century French art movement which propounded the merits of color over design.*
Rue	rue	*(Fr.) Street.*
Rue Amelot	...am **LO**	*(Fr.) A hard paste porcelain factory founded in 1786 on the Rue Amelot, Paris.*
Rue de Bondy	...duh boh(n) **DEE**	*(Fr.) A hard paste porcelain factory founded in 1780 on the Rue de Bondy, Paris.*
Rue de Crussol	...duh "crew" **SUL**	*(Fr.) A hard paste porcelain factory founded in Paris in 1789.*
Rue de la Roquette	...duh lah ruh **KET**	*(Fr.) An important mid-18th century ceramic center in Paris.*

Rue Fontaine-au-Roy	...foh(n) ten-oh-**RWAH**	*See La Courtille.*
Rue Popincourt	...poh pa(n) **KOOR**	*(Fr.) A hard paste porcelain factory founded in 1782 in Paris.*
Rue Thiroux	...tee **ROO**	*(Fr.) A hard paste porcelain factory founded at Paris in 1775, by Leboeuf.*
Rufous	**ROO** "fuss"	*Reddish pigment, similar to burnt sienna.*
Ruche	roosh	*Decorative trimming with pleated lace, net, ribbon, etc.*
Rustique	rue **STEEK**	*(Fr.) Any furniture made in the French provinces that is rough, coarse and unpolished.*
Rutakali	**ROO** ta **CAL** ay	*A type of horse blanket.*

R

S

Sabaton	**SAB** uh tahn	A 16th century broad-toed foot armor.
Saber	**SAY** ber	A slightly curved one-edged sword. Also, a type of curved front leg on a chair or sofa derived from the Greek klismos, typical of the Regency style.
Sabicu Wood	**SAB** uh koo	A West Indies hard wood resembling mahogany.
Sablier	sa blee **YAY**	(Fr.) An hourglass.
Sabot	sa **BOE**	(Fr.) In furniture, the applied decorative bronze shoemount at the base of a leg.
Sacellum	suh **KEL** um sah "**SELL**" um	A small chapel. In ancient architecture, a roofless shrine.
Sacra Conversazione	**SAH** krah con ver saht **SYOH** neh	(It.) A picture of the Virgin and Child with saints, arranged in realistic association with one another.
Sacra Famiglia	**SAH** krah fah **MEE** lyah	(It. 'holy family') A picture of the Virgin and Child accompanied by St. Joseph.
Sacrarium	suh **KRAHR** ee um	In architecture, a place in ancient temples where sacred vases and utensils were kept.
Sacring Bell	**SAY** cring	In ecclesiastical art, a small handbell.

Sacristy	"SACK" ri stee	An apartment in an ecclesiastical building in which the vestments and sacred vessels are kept.
Safronov	sah froh NOHF	(Rus.) A porcelain factory founded near Moscow in 1830.
Sagger or Seggar	SAG ur	A box or case of terra-cotta in which pieces of ceramic ware are placed and protected while baking.
Saibokuga	sah ee boh koo gah	A Japanese ink painting characterized by the traditional black with color.
Saint- Amand-les-Eaux	sa(n)t- a MAH(N)-lay-ZOE	(Fr.) A faïence factory founded here in 1718.
Saint Baume	sa(n) BOHM	A yellow-colored French marble with brown and red veining.
Saint Béat	sa(n) bay AH	A white French marble.
Saint-Clément	sa(n)-klay MAH(N)	(Fr.) A faïence factory founded here in 1758 as a branch of the Lunéville factory.
Saint-Cloud	sa(n)-"CLUE"	(Fr.) A soft-paste porcelain and faïence factory founded in the late 17th century at Saint-Cloud, Seine-et-Oise.
Saint-Jean-du-Désert	sa(n)-zhah(n)-due-day ZAIR	(Fr.) An early ceramic center founded in the 16th century at Saint-Jean-du-Désert near Marseilles.
Saint Mihiel	sa(n) mee "YELL"	(Fr.) An important lace-producing town in the province of Lorraine.
Saintonge	sa(n) TOH(N)ZH	A style of provincial furniture, named for a former French province.

S

Saint-Porchaire	sa(n)-"pour" "**SHARE**"	*(Fr.) An earthenware factory in St.-Porchaire, active around 1525. This ware is also called Henri Deux.*
Saint-Verain	sa(n)-vuh **RA(N)**	*(Fr.) A type of earthenware made in St.-Verain, Nièvre in the 17th century.*
Salade or Sallet	sa **LAD** "salad"	*A 15th century helmet used by foot-soldiers.*
Salière	sal **YAIR**	*(Fr.) A saltcellar.*
Salon d'Automne	sa **LOH(N)** "doe" "**TON**"	*An annual art exhibit in Paris, beginning in 1903.*
Salon des Indépendents	sa **LOH(N)** day za(n) day pah(n) **DAH(N)**	*An annual art exhibit in Paris, first held in 1884 by a group of painters opposed to the official salon.*
Salon des Refusés	sa **LOH(N)** day ruh "few" **ZAY**	*An art exhibition held in Paris in 1863 of paintings rejected by the official salon.*
Salopian	suh **LOPE** ee un	*In English ceramics, the name for a type of porcelain ware produced at Caughley.*
Saltire	**SAL** teer	*In heraldry, a special form of cross; e.g., a St. Andrew's cross.*
Samarkand	**SA** mer kand **SAH** mer kahnd	*An oriental rug of Turkoman classification.*
Same Yaki	sah meh yah kee	*(Jap.) A grey-colored ceramic ware resembling shark-skin.*
Samian Ware	**SAY** mee un	*An ancient type of Roman red-glazed pottery.*

Samite	**SAY** mite **SAM** ite	A heavy silk fabric worn in the Middle Ages.
Sandarac Wood	"**SAND**" uh "rack"	A hard, fragrant yellow-red wood of the Sandarac tree of northwestern Africa.
Sang de Boeuf	sah(n) duh **BU(R)F**	(Fr.'ox-blood') A deep red-glazed porcelain made in China during the K'ang Hsi period (1662-1722) onward. Also called Lang Yao.
Sang de Pigeon	sah(n) duh pee **ZHOH(N)**	A crimson-colored porcelain ware made in China possibly in the K'ang Hsi reign (1662-1722).
Sango-Toki	sahn go-toh kee	A Japanese manufactory of porcelain dinnerware founded in 1932 at Sango.
Sanguine	**SAN** gwin	A red chalk used in making drawings.
San To	sahn doh	(Chi.) The three fruits:peach, pomegranate, and persimmon.
San Ts'ai	sahn t"sigh"	(Chi.'three colors') Stoneware and porcelain enamelled in three colors, usually dark blue, turquoise, and aubergine.
Sapan Wood	suh **PAN** **SA** pan	A hard red wood of the Sapan tree of East India. Also, called Brazilwood.
Saph or Sarph, Saaph	sahf	Turkish family prayer-rugs characterized by multiple mihrabs.
Sapin Wood	sa pa(n)	A soft, white-colored fir tree.
Saraband Rug or Serebend	**SAR** uh band "**SARAH**" bend	An oriental rug of Persian origin.

S

Saracenic	sar uh **SEHN** ik	Pertaining to the Moorish style of architecture; e.g., Alhambra Palace in Granada, Spain.
Sarcophagus	sahr **KAH** fuh gus pl. -"guy"	A stone tomb usually with inscriptions and relief sculptures.
Sardonyx	sahr **DAH** nix	A hard, siliceous stone, used for cameos.
Sarreguemines	sahr guh **MEEN**	(Fr.) A large ceramic factory founded in Lorraine around 1770.
Saruk or Sarouk	suh "**ROOK**" sah **ROUK**	A closely knotted rug of Persian classification.
Satsuma	sat **SOO** muh **SAT** suh muh	(Jap.) A cream-colored pottery with a hard, crackled glaze, usually elaborately decorated in colors.
Satyr	**SAY** dur **SA** tur	A mythological figure with ears, legs, and horns of a goat. Often used on furniture from around 1730.
Sauna	"sow" nuh (as in "cow")	A Finnish steam bath.
Sautoir	so **TWAHR**	(Fr.) A long, gold neck chain, sometimes with a jewelled pendant.
Savignies	sa vee **NYEE**	(Fr.) A pottery center near Beauvais from the Middle Ages onward.
Savoie	sa **VWAH**	(Fr.) Pertaining to the French provincial furniture of Savoie.
Savona	sah **VOH** nah	(It.) A majolica center during the 17th and 18th century at this Ligurian coast town.

Savonarola Chair	sa vuh nuh **ROE** luh	*Italian Renaissance X-shaped wooden folding chair.*
Savonnerie Carpet	sa vun **REE**	*(Fr.) Knotted-pile "oriental" carpets manufactured at the Savonnerie factory founded in 1627 near Paris.*
Savonnette, Boîte à	sa vuh **NET** bwaht ah	*(Fr.) A soap box.*
Scabbard	"**SCAB**" urd	*A sheath for a sword or dagger.*
Scagliola	skal **YOE** luh	*An imitation marble made of plaster of Paris mixed with glue.*
Scarab	**SKA** "rub"	*A carved gem representing a beetle.*
Scauper	**SCAW** pur	*A metal tool used in engraving.*
Sceaux	"so"	*(Fr.) A porcelain and pottery factory founded near Paris before 1748.*
Schäpergläser	**SHAY** pur **GLAY** zur	*(Ger.) Drinking vessels decorated in black enamel. The name is derived from Johans Schäper who decorated both glass and pottery (1621-70).*
Schema	**SKEE** muh pl. -tuh	*In drawing, a simple diagram or depiction.*
Schiavone	skyuh **VOE** nee	*A 16ᵗʰ century Venetian broad sword.*
Schizzo	**SKEET** soh	*(It.) A term for a preliminary sketch.*
Schleswig	shlayz veeg	*(Ger.) A faïence factory founded here in 1755.*
Schmelz	shmelts	*(Ger.) A name for agate glass.*

S

Schnabelkrug	**SHNAH** bel "**CROOK**"	*(Ger.) A Rhenish stoneware jug characterized by a long beak-like spout.*
Schnelle	**SHNELL**ᵘʰ	*(Ger.) A tall tankard, usually of stoneware.*
Schönwald	shurn vowlt	*(Ger.) A porcelain factory founded here in 1879.*
Schrattenhofen	**SHRAH** t'n **HOE** f'n	*(Ger.) See Oettingen-Schrattenhofen.*
Schraub-Flasche	shrowp-**FLAHSH**ᵘʰ	*(Ger.) A stoneware flask characterized by being 4 or 6-sided and having a metal screw stopper.*
Schrezheim	shrez hime	*(Ger.) A faïence factory founded here in 1752.*
Schwarzlot	shvahrts lot	*(Ger.) Painted decoration in black enamel used on faïence, porcelain, and glass.*
Schwerin	shvair **REEN**	*(Ger.) A faïence factory founded here in 1753 and still in existence.*
Scimitar	**SIM** uh der **SIM** uh tahr	*A curved sword with single-edged blade of oriental origin.*
Sconce	skahns	*A bracket for candles.*
Scotia	skoe shee skoe shuh	*A deep concave molding which casts a strong shadow.*
Scribanne	scree bahn	*A bureau or secretary cabinet pertaining to Dutch and Flemish cabinetwork.*
Scrimshaw	**SKRIM** shaw	*Carved or engraved whalebone or whale ivory.*

Scrinium	**SKRIN** ee um *pl.* -uh	A cylindrical container used by the ancients for holding papyrus rolls.
Scrutoire	"screw" **TWAHR**	A rarely used term applied to early forms of English writing furniture.
Scutum	**SKYOO** tum *pl.* -tie	A large oblong Roman shield.
Secco	**SEHK** "o"	In painting, the technique of painting a mural on dry plaster.
Secretaire	seh kruh **TAIR**	A bureau, writing desk, or secretary.
Secrétaire à Abattant	suh kray **TAIR** ah a ba tah(n)	(Fr.) A writing cabinet with a fall-front panel.
Secrétaire à Panse	...ah pah(n)s	(Fr.) A desk with a cylinder-front.
Secrétaire-Bibliothèque	...bee blee oh **TEK**	A desk characterized by an upper cupboard or cabinet section.
Secrétaire-Chiffonnier	...shi fuh "**NEAR**" ..."she" "fun" **YAY**	(Fr.) A high chest of drawers having a writing section.
Secrétaire en Tombeau	...ah(n) toh(m) **BOH**	(Fr.) A desk characterized by a slant-front.
Section d'Or	sek syoh(n) "**DOOR**"	(Fr.'golden section') The name of an exhibition held in Paris in 1912 by a group of French Cubist painters.
Sedilia	seh **DEE** lyah	(It.) Stone seats in a church on the south side of the chancel used for clergy.
Sedjadeh or Sedjades	suh **JAH** duh **SED** ja dees	Iranian term for floor covering. Also, a rug measuring approx. 4 X 7 feet.
Sehna or Senneh	**SEN** nuh sen **NAY**	A Persian knotting technique. Also, the former name of a town (now Sanandaj) famous for its woven rugs and kelims.

S

Seicento	"say" **CHEN** toh	(It.) Pertaining to the Italian art period 1600-1700.
Seiji	seh ee jee	In Japanese ceramics, a term pertaining to a type of celadon.
Seillage	seh **YAHZH**	(Fr.) A type of French provincial cupboard.
Sejant	**SEE** junt	In heraldry, a seated animal with forelegs upright.
Semainier	suh men **YAY**	(Fr.) A tall narrow chest of seven drawers.
Semé	suh **MAY**	In heraldry, a shield covered with many small, identical figures.
Semerlik	seh mair "**LICK**"	Perso-Turkish word for saddle cover.
Sentoku	sen toh koo	A type of Japanese bronze.
Sepia	**SEE** pee uh	A brown-colored pigment derived from cuttlefish ink.
Seppa Dai	sep pah dah ee	In Japanese sword mounts, the oval space in the center of a tsuba around the opening for the tang.
Sepulcher or Sepulchre	**SEP** ul kur **SEP**'l kur	A tomb or burial place.
Serapeum	"Sarah" **PEE** um	A temple or building dedicated to Serapis in ancient Rome.
Serape or Sarape Serapi	seh **RAP** ee suh **RAH** pee	A blanketlike shawl or wrap. Also, an oriental rug of Persian origin.

Serif	**SER** if	A small cross-line or embellishment that finishes off the main stroke in a letter.
Serigraphy	si **RIG** ruh fee	Silk-screen printmaking.
Serpentine	"**SIR**" pen teen "**SIR**" pen tine	In cabinetmaking, having a convex center flanked by concave curves at each end.
Serre-Bijoux	sair-bee **ZHOO**	(Fr.) A jewel box or case on a table stand.
Serre-Papiers	sair-pa **PYAY**	(Fr.) An open-faced article of furniture with compartments and pigeonholes for papers.
Servante	sair **VAH(N)T**	(Fr.) A portable serving table.
Seto Ware	seh toh	(Jap.) Ceramic ware produced in the Seto district in the Owari province.
Settecento	seh teh **CHEN** toh	(It.) Pertaining to the Italian art period 1700-1800.
Settee	seh **TEE**	A seat for two or more persons, often with an upholstered back, seat and arms.
Setzbecher	**ZETS BEH** "care"	(Ger.) A type of small cup, usually of silver.
Sèvres	**SEV**ruh	(Fr.) A porcelain factory founded in 1738 at the Château de Vincennes.
Sfregazzi	sfreh **GAH** tsee	(It.) A painting technique in which the fingertips apply glaze over flesh tones.
Sfumato	sfoo **MAH** toh	(It.'smoke') In painting, a hazy, atmospheric effect achieved by a gradual change in color or value.

Sgabello	zgah **BEL** lo skah	(It.) A type of Renaissance side chair.
Sgraffiato or Sgraffito	zgrah fee **AH** toe sgrah **FEE** toe pl. -tee	(It. 'scratched') A scratched design through an overglaze to reveal a contrasting color.
Shagreen	sha "**GREEN**"	Untanned leather with granular indentations prepared from the skin of a donkey, horse, shark, etc.
Shah Abbas	shah uh **BAHS**	In rugs, an intricate floral pattern named after a Persian ruler.
Shakudo	shah koo doh	(Jap.) In metal art, an alloy consisting of 97% copper and 3% gold.
Shawabty Figures or Ushabti	shuh **WAB** tee "you" **SHAB** tee	Egyptian funerary figurines placed in the tombs.
Shen-lung	shun-lohng	(Chi.) A spirit dragon.
Shibayama	shee bah yah mah	(Jap.) A decorative technique on a lacquer ground using mother-of-pearl and other materials.
Shibuichi	shee boo ee chee	(Jap.) In metal art, an alloy used for decorative purposes.
Shibuichi-Doshi	shee boo ee chee-doh shee	(Jap.) A form of metal art.
Shigaraki	shee gah lah kee	(Jap.) An early important pottery center at Shigaraki in the Shiga prefecture.
Shingen Tsuba	sheen ghen tsoo bah	(Jap.) A type of tsuba with silver and copper wires woven over and through a plate of brass or iron.

Shino	shee noh	(Jap.) A type of ceramic ware from the kilns in the Mino province (late 16th century and early 17th century).
Shino Yaki	shee noh yah kee	(Jap.) A type of ceramic ware from the late 16th century.
Shiraz *or* Sheraz	shi **RAHZ** sheh **RAZ**	An oriental rug of Persian origin.
Shirvan	shur **VAHN** **SHUR** van	An oriental rug of Caucasian origin.
Shisham	**SHEE** shum	A brown-colored hardwood of the East Indies. Also, called Sissoo.
Shishi	shee shee	(Jap.) A Chinese mythological creature of a lion/dog combination.
Shitogi Tsuba	shee toh ghee tsoo bah	An early form of guard found on the ceremonial sword.
Shochikubai	shoh chee koo bah ee	(Jap.) Three lucky symbols: pine, bamboo, and plum.
Shoji	shoh jee	(Jap.) A type of sliding door or screen.
Shonzui *or* Shonsui	shohn tzoo ee	(Jap.) A porcelain ware named after the 16th century potter Gorodaiyu Shonsui.
Shou	"show"	In Chinese art, the character meaning long life.
Shou Lao	"show" low (as in "cow")	In Chinese art, a Taoist god of long life, and represented as an old man.
Shu Fu Ware	shoo foo	A Chinese porcelain ware produced at Ching-te-Chên for the Court of the Yüan Emperors (1280-1368).

S

Shun Chih	sh^{ue}en j^{uh}	*(Chi.) A reign of the Ch'ing Dynasty (1644-1661).*
Shu-Nuri	shoo-noo lee	*The Japanese name for red lacquer or cinnabar.*
Siamoise	syam **WAZ**	*(Fr.) Late 19th century double armchair or upholstered sofa named after the Siamese Twins (1811-1874). Also known as Tête-à-Tête or Vis-à-Vis.*
Sibyls	**SIB** ulz	*In ecclesiastical art, mythological creatures associated with the prophets as seen in the stained glass of the Middle Ages.*
Siegburg	zeek boork	*(Ger.) A pottery center at Siegburg in the Rhineland from the 14th century.*
Siena	see EN uh	*(It.) In ceramics, a pottery center at Siena, Tuscany as early as the 13th century. Also, a rich yellow-toned marble found mostly in France.*
Sigil	**SIJ** il	*A signet or seal.*
Silesia Hafner Ware	"sigh"**LEE** zhuh suh **LEE** shuh **HAHF** nur	*(Ger.) 16th century tin-glazed dishes made in Silesia.*
Silhouette	sil ou **ET** seel **WET**	*A profile of an object cut out of black paper or filled in with a solid color.*
Silla	shil lah	*A Korean historical period (57 B.C.–A.D. 935).*
Sillón de Caderas	see **YOHN** day kah **DAY** rahs	*(Sp.) A medieval X-form folding chair often richly decorated.*
Simpulum	**SIM** pyoo lum *pl.* -la	*An ancient ceremonial ladle.*

Sinceny	sa(n) suh **NEE**	(Fr.) A faïence factory founded in 1733 at Sinceny.
Singerie	sa(n) **ZHREE**	(Fr.) A decorative composition incorporating ape and monkey figures.
Sinkiang	sheen jᵉᵉahng sin kie ang	Rugs named after this Chinese province.
Sinopia	si "**NO**" pee uh	A red pigment, used from antiquity to the Middle Ages.
Sinumbra	si **NUM** bruh	A sperm-oil lamp.
Sipiagin	see **PYAH** ghin	(Rus.) An early 19ᵗʰ century porcelain factory near Moscow.
Sisal	"**SIGH**"s'l sis'l "**SEE**"s'l	A strong, durable fiber.
Sissoo *or* Sissu	**SIS** soo	A brown-colored hardwood from East India.
Sistrum	**SIS** trum	An ancient Egyptian musical instrument.
Situla	**SICH** uh luh **SIT** ᵘʰ luh *pl.* -lee	An ancient vase or deep urn.
Skiver	"**SKY**" vur	A thin soft leather.
Skyphos *or* Scyphus	"**SKY**" fahs **SKEE** fohs *pl.* -foy	(Gk.) An ancient two-handled drinking vessel.
Smaltino	smahl **TEE** no	(It.) A 16ᵗʰ century term for a pale blue or greyish tin-glaze found on majolica.
Smalto	**SMAHL** toe **ZMAHL** toh	(It.) Colored glass used in mosaic.

S

Snaphance or Snaphaunce	**SNAP** hance **SNAP** hahns	An early Dutch firelock.
Socle	"**SOCK**" 'l "**SOAK**" 'l	A base or pedestal.
Sofa à Pommier	suh **FAH** ah pum **YAY**	(Fr.) A massive type of Empire sofa.
Soleret	sul **REH**	(Fr.) In armor, pointed shoes of plate armor worn in the 14th century.
Sölvesborg	**SEL** ves **BOHR**	(Swe.) A faïence factory founded here in 1773.
Some Nishiki	soh meh nee shee kee	(Jap.) A porcelain technique using an underglaze blue and overglaze colors.
Sometsuke	soh meh tsoo keh	(Jap.) The term used for under-glaze blue and white porcelain.
Sopraporta	**SOH** prah **POR** tah	(It. 'overdoor') A pediment or painting found over a doorway.
Soroimono	"solo" ee moh noh	(Jap.) A term applied to a set of uniform objects; e.g., the fittings for a sword.
Sotto in sù	**SOH** toh in "**SUE**"	(It.) The extreme foreshortening of figures found in ceiling paintings.
Souj-Bulak	sah wooj-boo lagh	An oriental rug of Persian origin.
Soumak or Sumac	"**SUE**" mac	An oriental rug of Caucasian origin.
Soupière	"soup" **YAIR**	(Fr.) A vase or urn form usually found on Louis XVI and Empire furniture.

Sphene	sfeen	A gemstone, usually found in small wedge-shaped crystals.
Sphinx or Sphynx	sfinks	An imaginary creature having the head of a man or animal and the body of a lion.
Spinel	"SPIN" 'l spi NEL	A gemstone, characterized by hardness and octahedral crystals.
Spline	spline	A narrow flexible strip used as a ruler in drawing curved lines.
Spontoon	spahn TOON	In arms, a broad-bladed weapon.
Sprezzatura	spreh tsah TOO rah	(It.) In art, a drawing or sketch having a quality of studied carelessness.
Squeegee	SKWEE jee	In silk screen and serigraphy, an implement used to force paint through a porous surface or screen.
Squelette Clock	skuh LET	A type of clock whose works are exposed. Also called a skeleton clock.
Staatliches Bauhaus	SHTAHT leek "us" BOW "house"	A German school of design founded in 1919 by Walter Gropius.
Staffage	sta FAHZH	(Fr.) In landscape painting, the addition of figures as a secondary element.
Stalactites	STAL uk "tights" stuh LAK "tights"	In architecture, decoration suggesting the appearance of the petrified deposits hanging from caves and grottoes.
Stamnos	STAHM nohs	An ancient Greek storage jar.

S

Stanchion	**STAN** shun	An upright steel bar, post, or support for a girder.
Stangenglas	shtahn(g) en "glass"	(Ger.) A 17th century type of cylindrical beaker.
Statant	"**STAY**" tint	In heraldry, an animal, usually a lion, with all feet on the ground.
Steatite	**STEE** uh "tight"	Soapstone, used for carving.
Steingut	shtine goot	(Ger.) In ceramics, a lead-glazed ware.
Steinzeug	shtine tsoyk	(Ger.) In ceramics, a term for stoneware.
Stele	**STEE** lee "steel"	An upright slab of stone bearing an inscription or carved in relief.
Stellate	**STUH** late **STEL** it	In ornament, star-shaped.
Stereochromy	**STEER** ee uh "crow" mee	A method of mural painting. Also, called waterglass painting.
Steuben Glass	"**STEW**" ben "stew" **BEN**	American handmade lead crystal made by the Steuben Glass Works, Corning, N.Y.
Stiacciato	styah **CHAH** toh stee ah chee **AH** toe	(It.) In sculpture, a form of very low relief as found on coins.
Stigmata	**STIG** muh tuh stig **MAH** tuh	Marks resembling the wounds of Christ.
Stiletto	sti **LET** oh	A short dagger.
Stockelsdork	**SHTAHK** kuls **DORF**	(Ger.) A faïence factory founded here in 1771.
Store Kongensgade	**STOW**ah **KOHN(G)**enz **GATH**uh	(Dan.) A faïence factory established in Copenhagen in 1722.

Stoup	"stoop"	A shallow vessel for holy water.
Strasbourg	**STRAHS** burg **STRAHZ**	(Fr.) A faïence factory founded in 1720 at Strasbourg, Alsace.
Striation	s"try" "**A**" shun	A pattern of parallel grooves or lines.
Stupa	"**STEW**" puh	An artificially constructed mound of earth or stone containing a relic chamber.
Sturzbecker	**SHTURTS BEH** "care"	(Ger.) A stoneware or metal drinking cup with a stem in the form of a man.
Style Mécanique, le	"steel" may ka **NEEK**, luh	(Fr.) An early stage of Purism. Fernand Léger was its best known exponent(1881-1955).
Stylobate	"**STY**" luh "bait"	In architecture, a platform forming the foundation for a colonnade.
Stylus	"**STY**" lus pl. -lie	Any small pencil-shaped instrument used for incising lines.
Sudarium	soo **DAR** ee um pl. -uh	In ancient times, a cloth for wiping the face.
Suiboku	"sue" ee boh koo	(Jap.) A monochrome ink painting on silk or paper.
Sumi	"sue" mee	(Jap.) Black ink.
Sukashi-Bori	"sue" kah shee-boh lee	(Jap.) A decorative chiselling technique on metal.
Sultanabad	sul **TAN** a bad	An oriental rug of Persian origin.
Sumi-Ye	soo mee-yeh	(Jap.) Black ink pictures.
Sumi-Zōgan	soo mee-zoh gahn	(Jap.) In metal art, a term meaning ink inlaying.

S

Suprematism	soo **PREH** muh **TIZ'M**	A Russian art movement founded in 1913, deriving its geometrical form from Cubism.
Surcoat	"**SIR**" "coat"	Any garment worn over medieval defensive armor.
Sureau Wood	"sue" **ROE**	A hard yellow wood of the elder tree.
Surimono	soo lee moh noh	(Jap.) Prints used for special greetings or occasions.
Surplice	"**SIR**" plis	A white, loose-fitting garment worn by clergy and choristers.
Surrealism	"sir" **REE** uh liz'm "**SIR**" ree uh liz'm	An art movement founded by André Breton in 1924, characterized by an irrational, noncontextual arrangement of material.
Surtout	"sir" **TOO**	(Fr.) An ornamental centerpiece.
Suzuri Bako	soo tzoo lee bah koh	(Jap.) An ink-stone box.
Swage	swayj	A decorative border of grooving or molding.
Swansea	"**SWAN**" zee	The Cambrian Pottery in Swansea, Glamorganshire, Wales was active from 1765.
Swastika	**SWAHS** ti kuh swah **STEE** kuh	An ancient religious symbol or or ornamentation.
Swatow	**SWAH** tow	A type of Chinese export porcelain ware.
Synagogue	**SIN** uh gahg	A Jewish place of worship.
Synchronism	"**SING**" kruh niz'm	An early 20th century movement led by American painters.

Synthetism	"**SIN**" thuh tiz'm	*A style of painting adopted by Paul Gauguin and other artists during the period 1886-90 at Pont-Aven in Brittany.*
Systyle	**SIS** "tile"	*In architecture, an edifice having an intercolumniation of two diameters.*

S

T

Tabachi	tah **BAH** chee	A poor quality wool from dead animals.
Tabard	**TAB** urd	A medieval outer garment worn by a knight over his armor.
Table	**TA** bl^uh	(Fr.) Table
Table à Bijoux	...ah bee **ZHOO**	(Fr.) A table used for keeping jewelry.
Table à Coiffeuse	...ah kwah **FU(R)Z**	(Fr.) See Poudreuse
Table à Déjeuner	...ah day zhu(r) **NAY**	(Fr.) A breakfast table.
Table à Écran	...ah ay **KRAH(N)**	(Fr.) A table fitted with a screen.
Table à Écrire	...ah ay **KREER**	(Fr.) A writing table.
Table à Gradin	...ah gra **DA(N)**	(Fr.) A lady's small writing table with a recessed superstructure.
Table à Manger	...ah ma(n) **ZHAY**	(Fr.) A dining room table.
Table Ambulante	...ah(m) bue **LAH(N)T**	(Fr.) A portable table.
Table à Ouvrage	...ah oo **VRAHZH**	(Fr.) A small work table.
Table à Papillon	...ah pa pee **YOH(N)**	(Fr.) A small dressing table with mirror.
Table à Rognon	...ah roh **NYOH(N)**	(Fr.) A kidney-shaped table.
Table à Tronchin	...ah troh(n) **SHA(N)**	(Fr.) An architect's table.
Table-Bouillotte	...boo **YUT**	(Fr.) A card table with circular marble top.

Table de Chevet	...duh shuh **VAY**	(Fr.) A bedside table.
Table de Cuisine	...duh kwee **ZEEN**	(Fr.) A kitchen table.
Table de Jeu	...duh **ZHU(R)**	(Fr.) A gaming table.
Table de Lit	...duh **LEE**	(Fr.) A bedside table.
Table de Milieu	...duh mee **LYU(R)**	(Fr.) A center table.
Table de Nuit	...duh **NWEE**	(Fr.) A night stand.
Table Gigogne	...zhee **GUN**ʸᵘʰ	(Fr.) A nest of tables either graduated or of equal size.
Table-Guéridon	...gay ree **DOH(N)**	(Fr.) A medium or large circular table.
Table Liseuse	...lee **ZU(R)Z**	(Fr.) A reading table.
Taboret	**TAB** uh ret	A small cabinet to hold an artist's palette and supplies.
Tabouret	**TA** buh **RET** **TA** buh rit ta boo **REH**	(Fr.) A small stool without back or arms.
Tabriz Rug	tuh "**BREEZE**"	An oriental rug of Persian origin; a Persian city.
Taces	**TA** siz **TAYS** iz	See Tassets.
Tachi	tah chee	(Jap.) The earliest type of single-edged sword.
Tachisme	tah **SHEEZ**ᵐᵘʰ	(Fr.) A term used from the 1950's that corresponds to Action Painting.
Tachuelilla Wood	tah chweh **LEE** yah	A wood from Mexico, Costa Rica and South America, resembling poplar.

T

Taenia	**TEE** nee uh	In the Greek Doric order, the band that separates the frieze from the architrave.
T'ai Ch'ang	"tie" chahng	(Chi.) A reign of the Ming Dynasty (1620).
T'ai Po Tsun	"tie" boe tsoo[en]	(Chi.) A water vessel.
Taille d'Épargne	tah[yuh] day **PARN**[yuh]	(Fr.) Synonym of Champlevé.
Taka-Bori	tah kah-boh lee	(Jap.) Carving in relief.
Taka-Makie	tah kah-mah kee eh	(Jap.) A relief decoration in lacquer.
Takatori	tah kah toh lee	(Jap.) Pottery ware produced here from the late 16th century.
Taka-Zōgan	tah kah-zoh gahn	(Jap.) A decorative process of inlaying metal in relief.
Ta Kuan	dah gwahn	(Chi.) A variety of porcelain ware made at the Imperial potteries from the 12th century.
Talavera de la Reina	tah lah **BEH** rah deh lah **RAY** nah	(Sp.) Tin-glazed earthenware potteries founded here and in Castile in the mid-16th century.
Tambour	**TAM** bour	In furniture, a flexible sliding door for desks, cabinets, etc. In embroidery, a circular frame and a decorative stitch.
Tamisadou	tah mee sah **DOO**	(Fr.) A cupboard to hold the flour sifter.
Tanagra	**TAN** uh gruh tuh **NA** gruh	A small molded terra-cotta figure from ancient Greece.
T'ang	tahng	A Chinese dynasty (618-906).

Tanguile Wood _or_ Tangile	**TAHN** yuh lee "tan" **GHEEL**	A soft red-brown wood from the Phillipines.
Tansu	tahn soo	(Jap.) A mobile storage chest.
Tan-ye	tahn-yeh	(Jap.) Hand-colored pictures using a red lead pigment.
Tanzaku	tahn zah koo	(Jap.) Upright narrow prints measuring 14" X 6", inscribed with verses.
Tantalus	**TAN** tul us	An open-work rack for decanters, secured by a lock.
Tanzenmann	**TAHN** sen **MAHN**	A type of Swiss drinking vessel carved as a standing peasant, usually of wood.
Tao Kuang	dow gwahng	(Chi.) A reign of the Ch'ing dynasty (1821-1850).
T'ao T'ieh	tow t^{ee}eh	(Chi.) In art, a stylized dragon mask motif.
Taquillón	tah kee **YOHN**	(Sp.) In furniture, a type of decorative base used as a support for a vargueño.
Taracea	tah rah **SAY** ah	(Sp.) A type of inlay ivory decoration resembling grains of wheat.
Tarata Wood	tuh "**ROD**" uh	A tree of New Zealand used in cabinetwork.
Tassets	**TA** sits	In armor, over-lapping metal plates to protect the thighs. Also called taces.
Tatami	tuh **TAH** mee	(Jap.) A woven rice-straw mat about 3' X 6', used as a standard unit of measurement in a dwelling.

T

Tate-ye	tah teh-yeh	(Jap.) A term for upright pictures.
Tau	tow	A T-shaped cross, often called St. Anthony's cross.
Taufschein	towf shine	(Ger.) A baptismal certificate.
Tazza	**TAHT** suh	(It.) A shallow wine cup standing on a foot, and often with handles. Also, the raised basin of a fountain.
Tcherkess Rug	"chair" keez	An oriental rug of Caucasian origin.
Tchichi Rug	chee chee	See Chichi.
Tecalí	"take" ah **LEE** teh kah **LEE**	Mexican onyx.
Teinte	ta(n)t	French word meaning 'tint'.
Tegelen	tay <u>h</u>uh lun	(Dut.) An early pottery center founded here.
Tê-Hua	duh-whah	(Chi.) Factories located here made the white porcelain known as "Blanc de Chine."
Teheran	tay **RAN** tay **RAHN**	An oriental rug of Persian origin.
Tekke	**TEK** "key"	A major rug producing tribe of the Turkoman region.
Tekke Bakhara	**TEK** "key" boh **KAH** ruh ...boo **KAH** ruh	An oriental rug of Turkoman origin.
Telamon	tel uh **MAHN** pl. -**TEL** uh moe neez	A supporting column or pilaster carved in the form of a man.
Telesterion	tel uh **STEER** ee on pl. -ah	In ancient Greece, a ceremonial hall used to celebrate religious mysteries.

Temenos	**TEM** uh nahs **TEM** uh nus *pl.* -nee	A sacred enclosure around the Greek temple.
Temmoku	tem moh koo	*(Jap.)* A stoneware pottery with a dark brown glaze developed in China.
Tempera	**TEM** puh ruh	A painting technique in which the pigments are mixed with a glutinous substance soluble in water.
Tempyo	temp yoh	A Japanese time period (645-794).
Tenebrism	**TEN** uh briz'm	A painting technique that sub- merges figures in shadow but often illuminates the remaining forms.
Teocalli	tee o **KAL** lee teh oh **KAH** lee	*(Sp.)* In ancient Mexico, a type of pyramidal temple.
Tepesuchil Wood	ta peh **SOO** kil	A yellowish to brown-colored wood from tropical America.
Terra-Cotta	**TEH** ruh-**KAHT** uh	An unglazed brownish-orange baked clay. Also, a pigment resembling that color.
Terraglia	teh **RAH** lyah	*(It.)* Creamware or cream-colored earthenware.
Terrazzo	teh **RAHT** tsoh	*(It.)* A flooring material of marble chips set in cement, ground smooth and polished when dried.
Terra Sigillata	**TEH** rah see jee **LAH** tah	*(It.)* An ancient type of Roman pottery decorated with relief figures.
Terre de Lorraine	tair duh luh **REN**	*(Fr.)* A cream-colored pottery made at Lunéville.

T

Terre de Pipe	tair duh **PEEP**	(Fr.) A white-bodied ceramic ware with a lead glaze made at Lunéville.
Tertiary Colors	**TUR** shee **AIR** ee	Any hue created by mixing secondary colors together.
Teruel	teh roo **EL**	(Sp.) Tin-glazed earthenware factories produced here from the 13th-16th century.
Tessera	**TEH** suh ruh	The small tiles, marble, glass, etc. used in making a mosaic.
Testudo	teh "**STEW**" doe	In architecture, an arched roof or ceiling.
Tête-à-Tête	tet-ah-tet	(Fr.) An S-shaped, upholstered sofa for two persons. Also called Vis-à-Vis.
Tettau	tet tow	(Ger.) A porcelain factory founded here in 1794 and still in existence.
Theorem	thee uh rum	In painting, the process of using stencils and oil paint on velvet cloth.
Thonet, Michael	thoe **NAY** toe **NAY** "**TON**" et	A Viennese furniture maker who perfected the bentwood process (1796-1871).
Thurible	**THUR** uh b'l	An incense burner.
Thuringia	thur **IN** jee uh tour **ING** ee ah	(Ger.) Porcelain and faïence factories founded in the region of Thuringia during the 18th century.
Thuya Wood	**THOO** yuh	A fairly hard, mottled brown wood from Africa.

Thyrsus	**THUR** suss *pl.* -"sigh"	A long, ivy-entwined staff tipped with a pine cone, carried by Bacchus and satyrs.
T'ien Ch'i	t^{ee}en chee	(Chi.) A reign of the Ming dynasty (1621-1627).
T'ien-lung	t^{ee}en-lohng	In Chinese ornament, a Chinese sky dragon.
T'ien Shun	t^{ee}en sh^{ue}en	(Chi.) A reign of the Ming dynasty (1457-1464).
Tikh	**TEE** kay	In rug-making, a tool with hooked end.
Tiki	**TEE** kee	In Polynesian mythology, the first man created. Also, an image of wood or stone used as an abode or embodiment of a god.
Tilleul Wood	ti **YURL** tee **YU(R)L**	A soft, pale greenish-yellow wood of the linden tree.
Tillowitz	tee loh veets	(Ger.) A porcelain factory founded here, near Flakenberg, Silesia in 1869.
Ti-lung	dee-lohng	In Chinese ornament, a Chinese earth dragon.
Tinaja	tee **NAH** <u>h</u>ah	An early unglazed earthenware storage vessel produced in Moslem Spain.
Ting	deeng	(Chi.) A type of Bronze Age cauldron.
Ting Yao	deeng yow	(Chi.) In ceramics, a white ware made at Ting Chou during the T'ang (618-906) and Sung (960-1279) dynasties.

T

Tinja	**TEEN** "<u>ha</u>"	(Sp.) A type of large ceramic oil jar from Seville.
Tobe	toh beh	(Jap.) In ceramics, Tobe ware first produced in the Ebime Prefecture in 1775.
Tobi Seiji	toh bee seh ee jee	(Jap.) In ceramics, a spotted celadon.
Tobreh	**TOE** bray	A term for a small, woven, hammock-shaped bag.
Togidashi	toh ghee dah shee	(Jap.) A decorative form of lacquer work.
Togidashi-Zōgan	toh ghee dah shee -zoh gahn	(Jap.) A form of metal inlay work.
Toile	twahl	(Fr.) Cloth; e.g., linen, canvas, etc. Also, a lace pattern resembling woven fabric.
Toiles de Jouy	twahl duh **ZHWEE**	(Fr.) A cotton fabric usually printed with pastoral or figural scenes in monochrome on a beige ground.
Tokmak	tohk **MAHK**	An oriental rug of Turkish origin.
Tokoname	toh koh nah meh	(Jap.) In ceramics, Tokoname potteries situated near Nagoya from the 12th century onward. Also, a niche to display art work found in houses and tea-ceremony rooms.
Tokugawa	toh koo gah wah	A Japanese time period (1615-1868).
Tôle	"toll"	(Fr.'sheet metal') Painted tinware.

Toledo	teh **LEE** "doe" toh **LEH** thoh	(Sp.) An active pottery center here during the 16ᵗʰ -18ᵗʰ century. Also, a finely-tempered sword or blade made in Toledo, Spain.
Tonder Lace	**TU(R)** nah	A bobbin lace characteristic of Danish needlework. Also, a linen.
Tondo	**TAHN** doe pl. -dee	A circular painting. Also, a sculptured plaque or medallion.
Tonlet	"**TON**" lit	In armor, a bell-shaped skirt of plates.
Topia	**TOE** pee uh	(It.) A large painting of a formal garden or landscape.
To-Ori-Nishiki	toh-oh ree-nee shee kee	A Japanese imitation of Chinese silk brocade.
Toranj or Turunji	toh ranj	A term given to prominent medallion designs used in oriental rugs.
Torbas	**TOR** bahs	A woven bag, often used on goats as saddlebags, app. 2'6" X 4.
Torchère	tor "**SHARE**"	(Fr.) A tall, decorative stand for a candlestick, generally in pairs.
Torchon	**TOR** shahn	An inexpensive coarse bobbin lace.
Toreutics	tuh "**RUDE**" iks	Relating to working on metal in relief or intaglio.
Torii	toh ree ee	(Jap.) A Shinto shrine's formal gateway.
Torsade	tor **SAHD** tor **SADE**	A hat ornament of twisted ribbon or cord.
Tortillon	tor dee **YAHN** tor tee **YOH(N)**	(Fr.) A small rolled-paper stump used to blend charcoal and pastel.

T

Tosa	toh sah	(Jap.) A school of painting founded by Tosa Motomitsu in the 15th century.
T'o T'ai	toh "tie"	(Chi.) In ceramics, eggshell porcelain.
Tou	doe	(Chi.) A stemmed ritual bowl, usually covered.
Touraine Tapestries	too **REN**	(Fr.) A weaving center in Tours from the 16th-18th century.
Tourbillion Movement or Tourbillon	tur "**BILLION**"	A watch movement.
Tournay Tournai	"tour" **NAY**	(Flem.) Porcelain and pottery factories founded before the mid-18th century at Tournay in Flemish Doornik, Belguim. Also, tapestry factories.
Tou-Ts'ai	doe-tsie	(Chi.) In ceramics, a term meaning contrasted colors.
Trachelium	"track" **EE** lee um	The part of the neck of a Greek Doric column.
Traite	tret	(Fr.) A type of low, provincial cupboard.
Trapunto	truh **POON** toe trah **POON** toh	(It.) A quilted design in high relief.
Trauschein	trow shine	(Ger.) A marriage certificate.
Travailleuse	tra va **YU(R)Z**	(Fr.) A lady's worktable or stand.
Treacle	"**TREE**" kul	In cabinetmaking, a projecting quarter round molding on the lower edge of a hinged lid.

Trecento	treh **CHEN** toh	(It.) Pertaining to the Italian art period (1200-1300).
Trefoil	**TREE** "foil"	A decorative motif composed of three lobes.
Trembleuse	trah(m) **BLU(R)Z**	(Fr.) A type of saucer, character-ized by a raised ring to hold the cup.
Trichterbecher	**TREESH** tur **BEH** "care"	(Ger.) A salt-glazed stoneware cup.
Tricoteuse	tree koh **TU(R)Z**	(Fr.) A knitting worktable.
Tric-Trac Table	"trick"-"track"	(Fr.) A backgammon table.
Tridarn Cupboard	"**TRY**" "darn"	A type of Welsh cupboard.
Trifid	"**TRY**" fid	Split into three by deep notches.
Trifid-End Spoon	"**TRY**" fid	(Eng.) A type of spoon with the handle divided into three parts by deep clefts.
Triforium	"try" "**FOE**" ree um pl. -uh	In architecture, a gallery or arcade above the nave in a cathedral or church.
Triglyph	"**TRY**" gliff	An architectural ornament for a Doric frieze.
Triptych	"**TRIP**" tik	A three-paneled painting or bas-relief on hinges.
Triton	"**TRITE**" 'n	In mythology, a half man, half fish sea-monster.
Trofei	troh **FEH** ee	(It.) A term applied to a type of motif used on Italian Renaissance majolica; i.e., musical instru-ments, armor, weapons, etc.
Trois Crayons, à	twah creh **YOH(N)**, ah	(Fr.) A drawing made with black, red and white chalks on toned paper.

T

Trompe l'Oeil	troh(n) **PLUR** "trump" **LU(R)**[yuh]	(Fr. 'deception of the eye') A term applied to a painting that appears very realistic.
Trousse	"truce"	(Fr.) A kit, case or receptacle for implements.
Trucage	true **KAHZH**	(Fr.) In painting, a forgery.
Truité	twee **TAY**	(Fr.) In ceramics, a type of crackle, reminiscent of trout scales found on porcelain glazes.
Trumeau	true **MOE**	(Fr.) A pier mirror, consisting of mirror and painting.
Truqueur	true **CUR**	(Fr.) In painting, a forgerer.
Ts'a Ts'ai	tsah tsie	(Chi.) In ceramics, the combination of several colors used to decorate enamelled porcelain.
Tsêng	dsung	(Chi.) A large pot-shaped ritual vessel.
Tsuba	tsoo bah	(Jap.) A sword-guard.
Tsui-Shiu	dsoo[ee]-sh[ee]oo	(Chi.) In lacquerwork, carving through to reveal the several layers of colored lace.
Tsun	dsoo[en]	(Chi.) A type of ritual wine vessel.
Ts'ung	tsohng	(Chi.) A ritual vase with circular neck and foot.
Tsurugi	tsoo loo ghee	(Jap.) The oldest form of sword used, characterized by a straight double-edged blade.
T'u	too	(Chi.) In decoration, a hare figure used in ceramics and art.

Tuilles	tweel	In armor, pointed thigh guards hanging from the breastplate.
Tulle	"tool"	In lace-making, a thin, fine, bobbin-made net.
Tulwar or Tulwaur	**TUL** wahr	In arms, the Indian sabre.
T'ung Chih	tohng j^{uh}	(Chi.) A reign of the Ch'ing dynasty (1862-74).
Tung Yao	dohng yow	(Chi.) In ceramics, a celadon kiln at Ch'ên-liu making Eastern ware or Tung Yao.
Tunicle	**TOO** "nickle"	An ecclesiastical vestment worn by subdeacons and bishops.
Tupelo Wood	**TOO** puh "low"	Gumwood; a grayish-white, medium hard wood.
Turkoman	**TURK** uh mun	A classification of oriental rugs woven in this region.
Turquoise	**TUR** "coy"z tur **KWAHZ**	(Fr.) A type of daybed of the Louis XV period. Also, a blue, bluish-green or greenish-gray semi-precious stone.
Tusche	toosh^{uh}	A fluid used in lithography.
T'u Ting	too deeng	(Chi.) In ceramics, an early coarser potted ware with a finely crackled yellow glaze.
Tyg	tig	An English pottery drinking cup of the 17th-18th century, having three or more handles.
Tympanum	**TIM** puh num pl. -nuh	The triangular space in a pediment, sometimes decorated.

T

Typography	tie **PAHG** ruh fee	The art and practice of printing with movable type.
Tzu Chin	ds^{uh} jeen	(Chi.) In ceramics, a crackled ware of the K'ang Hsi period (1662-1722).
Tz'u Chou	ts^{uh} "joe"	(Chi.) In ceramics, stoneware produced at Tz'u Chou, possibly as early as the Sui dynasty (589-618).
Tzu-T'an Wood	ds^{uh}-tahn	(Chi.) A hard, reddish-brown wood, a.k.a. red sandalwood or palissandre.

U

Uchiwa-ye	oo che wah-yeh	(Jap.) Fan-shaped pictures.
Ukiyo-e	oo kee yoh-eh	(Jap.) 17th-19th century art featuring mainly woodblock prints illustrating events of everyday life.
Uncial	**UN** "she" ul **UN** chul	A type of calligraphy used especially in early Greek and Latin manuscripts, characterized by rounded capital (majuscule) letters.
Unguentarium	un gwun **TA** ree um	An ancient glass container to hold unguents.
Uragawara	oo lah gah wah lah	(Jap.) The protective metal guard on a scabbard at the opening of the pocket for the koyuka.
Urbino	oor **BEE** noh	(It.) Important center of majolica from the 16th century.
Urushi-ye	oo loo shee-yeh	(Jap.) In lacquer work, the use of metal dust on lacquer prints for effect.
Ushabti	"you" **SHAB** tee	See Shawabty.
Ushak or Oushak	oo "**SHOCK**" **OO** "shack"	An oriental rug of Turkish classification.
Uso-Niku-Bori	oo so-nee koo-boh lee	(Jap.) Low relief carving.
Utrecht	**YOU** trekt	(Dut.) 17th century painters from Utrecht emulating the style of Caravaggio. Also, a type of velvet with a cut pile.

V

Vagireh Rug	vah ghee reh	An oriental rug of Persian origin.
Vaisseau à mât	veh soh ah **MAH**	(Fr.) A porcelain boat-shaped potpourri introduced at Sèvres around 1755.
Vaisselier	veh suh **LYAY**	(Fr.) A cabinet with open shelves above and cupboard below.
Vaisselier-Horloge	veh suh lyay-or **LUZH**	(Fr.) A cabinet (See Vaisselier) having a tall class clock incorporated in the upper section.
Valencia	vah **LEN** see ah	(Sp.) Important pottery center here from the 13th century onward.
Valenciennes	vuh len see **ENZ** va lah(n) **SYEN**	(Flem.) A fine linen pillow lace produced at Valenciennes.
Vargueno	vahr "**GAIN**" yoe	A richly decorated type of drop-front cabinet-desk.
Vasa Murrhina	**VAH** suh muh **REE** nuh	A late 19th century American art glass.
Vasiliki Style	vah see lee **KEE**	An ancient decorative process on ceramics from east Crete.
Veduta	veh doo **TAH**	(It.) An accurate painting, drawing or print representing a portion of a town or city.
Vedutà Ideata	veh doo **TAH** ee deh **AH** tah	(It.) A scene realistically rendered but with imaginary elements. Synonym of Capriccio.

Veilleuse	veh **YU(R)Z**	*(Fr.) A type of chaise longue. Also, a pedestal or stand for holding small objects.*
Vellum	**VEL** um	*Calfskin prepared for writing and illuminations.*
Vendée	veh(n) **DAY**	*A provincial furniture style of Vendée, France.*
Veneer	vuh "**NEAR**"	*A thin layer of wood glued to a surface.*
Ventail	**VEN** "tail"	*In armor, a 16th century face guard.*
Veranda	vuh **RAN** duh	*An open porch, usually roofed.*
Verdaccio	vair **DAH** cho vair **DAH** chee "o"	*A greenish color similar to umber, used by late medieval Italian painters.*
Verdigris	**VUR** di "grease" vair dee **GREE**	*(Fr.) A bluish-green patina formed on copper, brass, and bronze surfaces. Also, a bluish-green pigment.*
Verdose	"**FAIR**" "dose"	*A Persian weaving center known for its rugs of undyed wool.*
Verdure	vair **DUER**	*(Fr. 'greenery') A tapestry whose design represents mainly leafy plants.*
Veremin	**VAIR** ah min	*An oriental rug of Persian origin.*
Verism	**VI** riz'm **VEH** riz'm	*In art, the attempt to represent truth and reality, even the vulgar or repugnant subjects.*
Verlys	vair "**LEASE**"	*(Fr.) A type of decorative novelty glass.*

Vermeil	**VUR** mill vur "**MAIL**" vair **MEH**^{yuh}	A French term for gilded metal, usually bronze or silver.
Vernis Martin	vair **NEE** mahr **TA(N)**	An 18th century French varnish to imitate oriental lacquer.
Verre de Fougère	vair duh foo **ZHAIR**	The French equivalent to waldglas (a German glass of green color).
Verre Églomisé	vair ay "glow" mee **ZAY**	(Fr.) Glass decorated by paint or gilt on the back and then protected by varnish and/or another sheet of metal or glass.
Verrier	vair **YAY**	(Fr.) Hanging wall shelves used for drinking glasses.
Vert Antique Marble	vair ah(n) **TEEK**	A marble in shades of green from Larissa, Thessaly, Greece.
Vesica Piscis	vuh "**SIGH**" kuh **PIE** sis **VES** i kuh	(Lat. 'fish-bladder') An elliptical aureole. Synonym of Mandorla.
Vesperbild	ves pehr beelt	Synonym for Pietà.
Vide-Poche	veed-puhsh	(Fr.) A pocket fitted into the arm of a chair to hold personal articles.
Vieux Paris	vyu(r) pa **REE**	(Fr. 'old Paris') 18th century porcelain wares known to be made in the Paris kilns but without proper identifying marks.
Vignette	vee **NYET**	(Fr.) A decorative foliage design around a capital letter or picture in a manuscript.
Vinaigrette	vin uh **GRET**	A small ornamental box of silver or gold generally containing a perfumed sponge.

Vincennes	va(n) **SEN**	*(Fr.) A porcelain factory established at Vincennes in 1765.*
Vingt, les	va(n), lay	*(Fr. 'the Twenty') A group of twenty late-19th century avant-garde painters.*
Vinovo	vee **NOH** voh	*(It.) A porcelain factory established at Vinovo in 1776.*
Virtù	veer **"TOO"**	*(It.) A term for objects of art or curios.*
Vis-à-vis	**VEEZ**-uh-**VEE**	*(Fr.) See Tête-à-Tête. The nature*
Vitreous	**VI** tree us	*of or pertaining to glass.*
Vitrine	vee **TREEN**	*A glass display case or cabinet.*
Vitruvian Scroll	vi **"TRUE"** vee un	*An ornamental scroll motif resembling stylized waves.*
Volant	**VOE** lunt	*A reinforcing piece of plate armor for the brow of a helmet.*
Volkstedt	"folk" shtet	*(Ger.) A porcelain factory founded in 1760 at Volkstedt, Thuringia.*
Volute	vuhl **YUTE** vuh **LUTE**	*A spiral scroll used to ornament the capital of an Ionic column.*
Vorticism	**VOR** tuh siz'm	*A British art movement (1912-15), regarded as an offshoot of cubism and futurism.*
Vouge	voozh	*In armor, a type of pole arm.*
Voussoirs	voo **SWAHR**	*(Fr.) Wedge-shaped blocks that form an arch.*
Voyeuse	vwah **YU(R)Z**	*(Fr.) A type of upholstered conversation chair.*

V

Vrai Réseau   vreh ray **ZOE**   *(Fr.) A net ground in lace made with bobbins or with the needle.*

W

Wainscot	**WANE** skut **WANE** skaht **WANE** skote	Interior panelling in wood, especially as covering the lower portion of a wall.
Wakazashi	wah kah zah shee	The shorter of the two swords carried by a Japanese samurai.
Waldenburg	vahl den boork	(Ger.) Ceramic potteries established at Waldenburg, Saxony in the Middle Ages.
Waldglas	valt glahs	(Ger.) Green-colored utilitarian glass made from the early Middle Ages.
Wallendorf	**VAH** len **DORF**	(Ger.) A porcelain factory established at Wallendorf, Thuringia in 1764.
Walzenkrug	**VAHL** sun **KROOG**	(Ger.) A cylindrical drinking vessel.
Wampum	**WAHM** puhm	Cylindrical beads made from sea shells and used by the American Indians for multiple purposes.
Wan Li	wahn lee	(Chi.) A reign of the Ming dynasty (1573-1619).
Wari-Kogai	wah lee-koh gah ee	A split kogai on a Japanese sword mount.
Wassail Bowl	**WAH** sil **WAH** sail	A medieval bowl used in England.

Weesp	waspe	(Dut.) A porcelain factory founded at Weesp in 1759.
Westerwald	**VEST** er **VAHLT**	(Ger.) A district of the Rhineland famous for its stoneware factories.
Whieldon, Thomas	"**WHEEL**" dun	Notable English Staffordshire potter (1719-95).
Wiederkomm	**VEE** dur "**COME**"	(Ger.) A glass drinking vessel of the 16th-17th century.
Wiener Werkstätte	**VEE** nur **VAIRK** shtah tuh	A Viennese association of designers and craftsmen established in 1903.
Willkom	"veal" "come"	(Ger.) A glass drinking vessel of the 16th-17th century.
Winifred	**WIN** uh frid	A Welsh saint.
Worcester	**WOOS** tur	(Eng.) A porcelain factory founded at Worcester in 1751.
Wrisbergholzen	vrees bairk hohl tsun	(Ger.) A faïence factory established in Hanover around 1735-37.
Wu Chin Ware	oo jeen	(Chi.) A black glaze porcelain of the K'ang Hsi period (1662-1722).
Wu Ts'ai	oo tsie	(Chi. 'five colors') White Chinese porcelain decorated with enamels on the biscuit or overglaze.
Wyvern	"**Y**" vurn	In heraldry, an imaginary beast.

X

Xoanon	**ZOE** uh nahn *pl.* -nuh	*In ancient Greek sculpture, a simply carved statue.*
Xylography	zie "**LOG**" ruh fee	*The art of wood engraving.*
Xyst *or* Xystus	ziest **ZIS** tuhs *pl.* -tie	*In architecture, an ancient Greek and Roman hall or portico.*

Y

Yaki	yah kee	*In ceramics, the Japanese word for ware.*
Yallahmeh *or* Yalameh	**YAH** lah may	*A contemporary Iranian rug.*
Yamato-e	yah mah toh-ee	*The Japanese traditional painting style initiated in the 10th century.*
Yarkand	yahr **KAHND**	*An oriental rug from East Turkestan.*
Yataghan	**YAD** uh gan	*In arms, a long Turkish saber with a curved blade.*
Yatsushiro	yah tsoo shee loh	*(Jap.) A small pottery in the province of Higo.*
Yayoi	yah yoh ee	*Early Japanese ceramics named after a Neolithic site in Tokyo where it was first excavated.*
Ye-goyomi	yeh-goh yoh mee	*(Jap.) Pictorial calendars.*
Yehon	yeh hohn	*(Jap.) A picture book.*
Yesería	yeh seh **REE** ah	*(Sp.) An interior decorative carved plasterwork.*
Yew Wood	"you"	*A hard reddish wood of the Yew tree. Also called If wood.*
Yezd Rug	yazd	*An oriental rug of Persian classification.*

Yi	ree	A Korean historical period (1392-1910).
Yi Hsing Yao	yee sheeng yow	(Chi.) Potteries in Kiang-su province producing unglazed stoneware.
Ying-Ch'ing	yeeng-tseeng	(Chi.) In ceramics, a Sung dynasty ware (960-1279).
Ying-Hsiung	yeeng-shohng	(Chi.) A type of vase from the Ming period (1368-1643) with figures of a bear and an eagle.
Ying Ts'ai	yeeng tsie	A Chinese term for hard enamels.
Yin-Yang	yeen-yahng	In Chinese symbols, yin, the female element; yang, the male counterpart.
Yodansu	yoh dahn soo	(Jap.) A type of lacquered rectangular cabinet.
Yoko-ye	yoh koh-yeh	In Japanese prints, a term for horizontal pictures.
Yomud Rug or Yomut/Yamout	yoh **MOOD**	An oriental rug of Turkoman origin.
Yorkshire Chair	**YORK** "sure"	(Eng.) A type of oak side chair from the Jacobean period (1603-49).
Youghal	yawl	(Ir.) Linen needlepoint lace made at the Presentation Convent at Youghal, County Cork from 1852 onward.
Yokkaichi	yoh kah ee chee "you" kah ee chee yoe kah ee chee	(Chi.) A Bronze Age ritual wine vessel.

Y

Yü	"you"	(Chi.) A general term for jade.
Yüan	"U.N."	A Chinese dynasty (1280-1368).
Yu-ch'ui P'ing	yoe-ch^{ue}ay peeng	(Chi.) A club-shaped vase.
Yüeh Yao	y^{ue}eh yow	(Chi.) An early grey-bodied celadon ware.
Yung Chêng	yohng jung	(Chi.) A reign of the Ch'ing Dynasty (1723-35).
Yung Lo	yohng luh	(Chi.) A reign of the Ming Dynasty (1403-24).
Yuruk Rug or Yourouk	you rook you **ROOK**	An oriental rug of Anatolian origin.

Z

Zaffer	**ZAF** ur	In pottery, a term for cobalt blue used for painting underglaze.
Zara Maki	zah lah mah kee	(Jap.) In sword mounts, the surface texture imitating stone. See Ishime.
Zecchino	zeh "**KEY**" no tseh "**KEY**" no	(It.) Sequin.
Zeitgeist	**TSITE** "guy"st	(Ger. 'the spirit of the time') The name of an art exhibition of Neo-Expressionist paintings in Berlin in 1982.
Zenjan Rug	zan jahn	An oriental rug of Persian origin.
Zerbst	zairbst	(Ger.) A faïence factory founded in 1720 at Anhalt.
Ziggurat	**ZIG** guh rat	An Assyrian tower-temple in the form of a stepped pyramid.
Zodiac	**ZOE** dee ak	In architecture, referring to bas-reliefs representing signs of the zodiac.
Zōgan	zoh gahn	(Jap.) In sword mounts, a name pertaining to inlay work.
Zopfstil	tsohpf shteel	(Ger. 'pig-tail style') A term used for the mid-late 18th century Classic Revival style.
Zoophorus	**ZOE** "fur" us pl. -fuh "**RYE**"	In architecture, a frieze decorated with people or animals.

Zunftbecher	**TSOONFT BEH** "care"	*(Ger.) A type of late 17th century glass beaker.*
Zuni	"**ZOO**" nee	*Silver jewelry produced by the Zuni Indians of New Mexico.*
Zwiebelmuster	**ZVEE** b'l **MOOS** tur	*(Ger.) In porcelain decoration, a term meaning onion pattern.*
Zwischengoldglas	**ZVI** sh'n **GOLT GLAHS**	*A glass vessel having a laminated layer of gold encased in a sheath of glass.*

Bibliography

Adeline, Jules, *The Adeline Art Dictionary*. New York: Frederick Unger Publishing Company, 1966.

Aronson, Joseph, *The Encyclopedia of Furniture*. New York: Crown Publishers, 1965.

Baker, Lillian, *100 Years of Collectible Jewelry*. Paducah, KY: Collector Books, 1978.

Barnhart, Clarence L., *The American College Dictionary*. New York: Random House, 1956.

Boger, Louise Ade, *The Complete Guide to Furniture Styles*. New York: Charles Scribner's Sons, 1959.

Boger, Louise Ade and H. Batterson Boger, *The Dictionary of Antiques and the Decorative Arts*. New York: Charles Scribner's Sons, 1967.

Boger, Louise Ade, *The Dictionary of World Pottery and Porcelain*. New York: Charles Scribner's Sons, 1971.

Dizik, Allen A., *Concise Encyclopedia of Interior Design*. New York: Van Nostrand Reinhold, 1988.

Ehresmann, Julia M., *The Pocket Dictionary of Art Terms*, Second Revised Edition. New York: New York Graphic Society, 1979.

Elspass, Margy Lee, *North Light Dictionary of Art Terms*. Cincinnati: North Light Publishers, 1984.

Fairholt, F.W., *A Dictionary of Terms in Art*. Detroit: Gale Research Co., 1969.

Fleming, John and Honour, Hugh, *Dictionary of the Decorative Arts*. New York: Harper and Row, 1977.

Gloag, John, *A Complete Dictionary of Furniture*. Woodstock, NY: Overlook Press, 1991.

Haggar, Reginald G., *A Dictionary of Art Terms*. New York: Hawthorn Books, Inc., 1962.

Hainworth, Henry, *A Collector's Dictionary*. London: Routledge & Kegan Paul, Limited 1981.

Harling, Robert, *Studio Dictionary of Design and Decoration*. New York: Viking Press, 1973.

Hinckley, Lewis F., *A Directory of Antique French Furniture 1735-1800*. New York: Crown Publishers, 1967.

Love, Catherine E., *Webster's New World Italian Dictionary*. New York: Simon and Schuster, 1985.

Lucie-Smith, Edward, *The Thames & Hudson Dictionary of Art Terms*. London: Thames and Hudson LTD., 1984

Mayer, Ralph, *A Dictionary of Art Terms and Techniques*. New York: Thomas Y. Crowell Co., 1969.

Mollett, J.W., *An Illustrated Dictionary of Art and Archaeology*. New York: America Archives of World Art, Inc. American Library Color Slide Co., Inc., 1966.

Neff, Ivan C. & Carol V. Maggs, *Dictionary of Oriental Rugs*. New York: Van Nostrond Reinhold Co., 1979.

Newman, Harold, *An Illustrated Dictionary of Jewelry*. New York: Thames and Hudson, 1981.

Quick, John, *Artists' and Illustrators' Encyclopedia*, second edition. New York: McGraw-Hill, Inc., 1977.

Random House Dictionary of the English Language. New York: Random House, 1987.

Ripley, Mary C., *The Oriental Rug Book*. New York: Frederick A. Stokes Company, 1904.

Robert, Paul, *Le Petit Robert*. Paris: Le Robert, 1981.

Savage, George, *Dictionary of Antiques*. New York: Praeger Publishers, 1970.

Stone, George C., *A Glossary of the Construction, Decoration and Use of Arms and Armor in all Countries and in all Times*. New York: Jack Brussel Publisher, 1961.
Ulrich, Schürmann, *Oriental Carpets*. London: Paul Hamlyn, Limited, 1966.

Websters' Third New International Dictionary. Springfield, Massachusetts: G. & C. Merriam Company, Publishers, 1981.

Wingate, Isabel B., *Fairchild's Dictionary of Textiles*. New York: Fairchild Publications, 1979.

Typeset in Gill Sans by Eric Gill (1882-1940)
and P22 Johnston Underground,
based on the London Underground signage.

Book design by Sarah F. Bauhan
Printed by Thomson-Shore, Dexter, Michigan

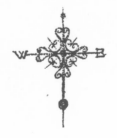